BYTES OF POETRY

A Lovestories.com Anthology

edited by Alanna Webb

Bytes of Poetry
A Lovestories.com Anthology

Copyright © 2000 Alanna Webb
First Printing October 1999

All rights reserved. All poems contained herein are copyrighted by the individual poets. No part of this book may be reproduced in any form without written permission of the poets and publisher except for the inclusion of brief quotations in a review or article.

Backup Computer Resources
905 South 30th Street
Broken Arrow, OK 74014
(918) 258-7669
http://www.lovestories.com
webmaster@lovestories.com

ISBN: 0-9676162-0-4

Printed in the U.S.A. by
Morris Publishing
3212 E. Hwy 30 • Kearney, NE 68847
1-800-650-7888

*to my parents, Olga and William Webb,
for their unending love and support*

CONTENTS

ACKNOWLEDGMENTS ix
INTRODUCTION x

Six-Year Old's View Of Kissing - *C.J. Heck* 1
The Flame - *T. J. Daniels* 2
Until The Day - *Jerry Chiccarine* 3
Peanutbutter Kisses - *Paula Duquette* 4
I Walk Alone - *Carrie L. Reger* 5
As Close As My Heart - *Grey Winds* 6
Moth And Flame - *Charles Albano* 7
It's A Guy Thing - *Chuck Pool* 8
10 Rules Of Love - *B.W. Behling* 10
Miracle On My Patio - *Sheila Cadilli* 12
Broken River Blues - *Butterfly Dreams* 13
A Silent God - *Carrie L. Reger* 14
Between Your House And Mine - *Martha Powell-Mitchell* 15
Breath Of Life - *Kelsey Blackmore* 16
Upon Meeting - *Jerry Chiccarine* 17
Blow Me A Kiss - *Bob Pool* 18
...And He Whispered (Dual Poems) - *C.J. Heck* 19
Love Unrequited - *C. Elizabeth* 20
The Actor - *~ Angel ~* 22
Everytime - *Brent Clayton Faust* 23
Do Lawd 'Member Me - *Randall Longshore* 24
She Happens To Be Beautiful - *Rod Smith* 26
Ransom Note - *Bryana Johnson* 27
Justice For All - *Grace Martino* 28
Powerful Love - *Pauline Hamblin* 31
The Rose - *Tammy S. Hoover* 32
Picnic For Two - *Brenda Mae* 34
My Little Guy - *Robert L. Macchia* 35
In My Hand - *Tony Spivey* 36
Just Three Words - *Butterfly Dreams* 38
Nature's Masterpiece - *Lydia Castilho* 39
Shadow Song - *Jim Morton* 40
Chalice Of Love - *wintersong* 41

Soul's Reward - *Renée Rose*	42
Moonlight - *~ Angel ~*	43
IF - *Basi Hummel*	44
Charmed - *Brenda Swanberg*	45
Just One Kiss - *Michael J. Tripp*	46
My Little Sister - *Bob Brokaw*	47
The Tree In My Own Backyard - *John Dee*	48
Finding Hope - *Dave Nieman*	49
What We Leave Behind - *Grey Winds*	50
...Well, You Know - *D. L. Frantz*	52
Keep To Your Heart - *John Dee*	53
The Necklace - *Dhynah*	54
Dreamin' ~ *Kathleen Kerry Swanson*	56
Sunrise - *Sunny Pierce*	57
Forever & A Day - *Tammy Lively-Sellers*	58
A Picnic With Shakespeare - *Christopher A. Smith*	59
Another Time, Another Place - *D. L. Frantz*	60
I Sometimes Think Dark Thoughts - *Amanda Piotrowski*	61
Always Daddy's Girl - *Andrea L. Michano*	62
Mirror - *wintersong*	63
When Love Could Be So Easy - *Jim Morton*	64
First Kiss - *Dale Edmands*	65
Another Ride? - *Dhynah*	66
Artist - *Brent Clayton Faust*	67
Hard Drive - *Jim Culhane*	69
Rain - *J.C. Monterrosa*	70
Love Is - *Anthony Limes*	72
Ode To A Cheeseburger - *Christopher A. Smith*	73
Trusted Love - *Max The Poet©*	74
To Say Good-bye To You - *Kathleen Kerry Swanson*	75
Silent - *Kathleen Kerry Swanson*	76
Old-Fashioned Guy - *Amun-Ra*	77
The Agony In A Teardrop - *T. J. Daniels*	79
Walk With Me To The Shoreline - *Jim Culhane*	80
My Travels - *Bob Brokaw*	82
Just As I Think - *Anthony Limes*	85
Casting Stones - *Julia Warfel*	86
Unspoken Words - *Maurice Sherry*	87

I'm A Guy - *John Henry Scott* 88
I.M.i.s.s.Y.o.u. - *Odessa Lynette Price* 89
Storms On The Ocean - *Julia Warfel* 90
He Let Me Hold His Hand - *Paula Duquette* 92
Poet To Poet - *Sandra Wommack* 93
Exile - *Randall Longshore & Elyse Ford* 94
Cold Champagne Dreams - *C.J. Heck* 96
In Love With You - *Dale A. Edmands* 98
So In Love With You - *Jim Morton* 99
We Kissed With Nature - *Rod Smith* 100
A Butterfly - *Paula Duquette* 101
Live On (Peter's Poem) - *Julia Warfel* 102
Describing Heaven - *Danny Grubb* 103
Thirty Years Of Waiting For Real Love - *Brenda Bailey* 104
A Dance - *Kimberlee Haines* 106
Honey, I'm Late - *Merrie Wilbanks* 107
Flower Among the Weeds - *Hal Gantt* 108
Mr. & Mrs. Haid - *Susan Fridkin* 109
Child, Girl, Woman - *Maria Y. Kurland* 110
Elysium - *James H.K. Grannis* 111
I Am Leaving - *Shawn Hayden Ramsingh* 112
The Journey - *Danny Grubb* 113
Forever For Tonight - *Caitlin R. Lee* 114
Time Well Spent - *Elyse Ford* 115
My Noble Grandmother - *Marnie L. Pehrson* 117
Faded Lust - *Merrie Wilbanks* 118
Cinderella's Broken Slipper - *Elyse Ford* 119
Our Little Picnics - *Nancy Jones* 120
Sweet & Yet... So Simple - *Monica Therese Curran* 122
2:00am - *Kevin Drapela* 123
The Light Inside - *Lynette Webber* 125
Belong To Thee - *Shawn Hayden Ramsingh* 126
Ode To Feminism: Humankind Is Here - *Bill Sterling* 128
Butterflies Of Saturn - *Suzanne Delaney* 129
Missed Connections - *Tony Kinard* 130
I Know - *Lynette Webber* 132
A Blanket Full Of Dreams - *Robyn Doersam* 133
Fool Of Infiniti - *Suzanne Delaney* 134

Under All That - *Katie Backus* 136
Starting Anew - *Debbie Gooch* 137
The Screen - *Emerson Dawson* 138
Portraits - *Hal Gantt* 139
Baby's Blessing - *Julia M. Zwicker* 141
Closing Doors - *Alanna Webb* 142

ABOUT THE POETS 144
INDEX OF POETS 152
ABOUT THE EDITOR 154
LOVESTORIES.COM POETRY COMMUNITY 155

ACKNOWLEDGMENTS

First, and foremost, I wish to thank all the poets whose poetry is featured in this book. Your poetry has shaped its personality. And, to all of the poets who have posted at Lovestories.com: Don't lose heart if your poetry wasn't selected. We have plans to print many more volumes, and your poetry could be featured next!

Thank you to Jodi Turek and all the wonderful people at The Women's Forum (http://www.womensforum.com). We appreciate all the support we've received since joining their network of web sites. The Women's Forum is *the network for women & girls of all ages*.

Special thanks to Cathy Stucker for her assistance in reviewing our manuscript and promotional materials. Cathy, the Idea Lady™ (http://www.idealady.com) specializes in helping entrepreneurs, authors and professionals create innovative information products and find creative ways to promote themselves and their businesses.

Thank you to Marlow Peerse Weaver (*In Our Own Words: Generation X Poetry*) and Judy Gripton (*The Amateur Poetry Journal* web site) for their input during our initial work on this book.

Sincere thanks to Becky Parish for all of her patience and attention and to all the people at Morris Publishing. They made it a positive experience to publish our first book. We look forward to working with them again soon.

I have wonderful, dear friends, too many to list here, but I want all of you to know that I appreciate your support. Last, but not least, I thank my parents, Olga and William Webb, who have been there for me from the inception of Lovestories.com, through all the growing pains and achievements, to the printing of this book, a personal dream of mine ever since I founded the site. Rock on!

INTRODUCTION

"At the touch of love, everyone becomes a poet." - Plato

After opening Lovestories.com web site in September 1997, it was immediately obvious that poetry would be one of our most popular sections. Six months later, we automated it when we couldn't keep up with posting the poems manually. In just one year, over 40,000 poems had been posted, and both visitors and poets alike enjoy reading new poems every day.

We provide free Poet Accounts, allowing anyone with Internet access to post original poetry on the Internet. Poets love it. They can log in anytime, 24 hours a day, 7 days a week, to post, edit, or delete poems. Lovestories.com poetry community is one of the largest on the Internet. But, it goes beyond numbers. It's an indication of how popular poetry has become. Who says that poetry is a lost art? Tell that to the millions of visitors our site receives every year!

What we find so satisfying is that Lovestories.com is providing a platform for people of all ages and varying races, religions, politics, etc. to relate together through poetry. Our poetry community is interactive for poets and visitors, with comment forms, chat, and message boards. Friendships have developed, and even a few romances. In fact, two of the poets in this volume met through our poetry community and are now sharing a new life. Plus, the poets also include two brothers, and an aunt and niece. The common bond among all the poets is their mutual love of poetry.

Many people have asked us to publish poetry books so the poetry can be enjoyed offline. What a wonderful idea, especially considering how difficult it is as an individual poet to get his/her poetry published through traditional publishing houses. Right from the start we had specific goals in mind for this anthology:

- to promote poetry to the masses
- to showcase as many poets from Lovestories.com as possible
- to publish a book that will appeal to a wide range of people

Our primary goal is to promote poetry both from the readers' and the poets' perspectives. With that in mind, we decided to print a book that would be inexpensive, in an informal design that would encourage people to carry it anywhere to enjoy poetry on a daily basis.

While proper grammar and spelling are important, both played a small part in the poem selection. A poem was selected based on its effect on readers, not whether it was perfect in structure. We wanted the poetry to whet the readers' appetite and enjoyment for poetry.

This anthology is the first of what we plan to be many volumes. It reflects a wide variety of poems with topics ranging from love and romance to nature, family, friendship, social issues, heartbreak, divorce, jealousy, inspiration, hope, and more. We selected a few poems initially, and then asked these poets to nominate their favorite poems. Then, we asked those poets to nominate, and so on, so this anthology is a mixture of tastes and preferences of many people, not just our staff.

The poems were selected without regard to age, gender, race, or anything beyond the poems themselves. But funny enough, the poets represent a wide cross-section of people: the gender is evenly split male/female, and the age of the poets range from 14 to 65+ with a fairly even distribution among the generations. The poets range from several who have been writing poetry for years, to those who started writing after visiting our site. Some poets have been published before, but for most, this is their first publishing opportunity, and we hope that they will have other opportunities to share their poetry as a result.

On a personal note, many people have asked to read my poetry. Even though I have a technical background in engineering, I have always been interested in English and creative writing. I haven't written poetry since highschool, but how can I truly appreciate the vulnerability of our poets without sharing my own poetry? So, I sat down and wrote a poem entitled "Closing Doors" and included it at the back of this book. I found it personally satisfying so I plan to write more.

This book is meant to be read and re-read. It's our hope that you will return to enjoy the poetry again and again, share it with friends and family, read poetry to your sweetheart, and that you will be inspired to write poetry yourself. Just for fun, I invite you to read the poems first, then try to guess the poets' ages and backgrounds before peeking at their bios in the back. I found it impossible to guess correctly...

If you enjoy the poems in this anthology, please take a few minutes to write the poets. I'm sure they will appreciate it. We have posted a special web page at:
http://www.lovestories.com/templates/volume1.cfm
where you can email comments to the poets and keep up with our latest news and information.

So what are you waiting for? Hours of reading pleasure is just a page turn away!

– Alanna Webb

Six-Year Old's View Of Kissing

I like to kiss my mommy,
Sometimes my daddy, too.
My brother kisses everything
'Cause that's what babies do.

I draw the line at kissing
With Mom and Dad, that's cool.
But, I run as fast as I can go
When the girls chase me at school!

C.J. Heck

The Flame

I felt like a moth
fluttering around a flame,
Afraid to leave,
yet afraid to stay.

I had a burning desire...
lost all my senses,
And was trapped behind
many unseen fences.

What to do now? I had not a clue.
Finally decided
'tis better to move.

I moved from the flame
and felt safer somehow...
'Tis much colder here,
but more protected now.

T. J. Daniels

Until The Day

Ah my sweet! Your effervescent
    Words could hell disarm.
    I find myself quite tempted
    To surrender to your charm.

    Know this! I do implore,
      Though we be apart,
Across the gap that divides us,
Your beauty has won my heart.

Until the day, we are together,
    I'll in patience wait.
Until then, from afar, I'll admire,
    And put my trust in fate.

    Jerry Chiccarine

Peanutbutter Kisses

He races in bringing
a rugful of mud
and smiles so sweetly
when he hands me a bug

Watching him grow is both
wonderment and chore
as he disassembles the house
in the middle of the floor

Pillows and blankets
and four kitchen chairs
so quickly can turn
to dungeons and lairs

Sunsets and rainbows
discovered brand new
the promise of Jesus
so simple and true

There are days
when his sunshine
turns quickly to rain
and moments so beautiful
I'll never capture again

One day he'll find her
and I'll be replaced
still feeling peanutbutter kisses
planted on my face

Paula R. Duquette

"for my firstborn, Alex Patrick, who is one of my treasures beyond compare."

I Walk Alone

There's a special place I love to go
It holds memories sweet and tender
Life was good and love was real
But now, I just remember

I walk alone in rain or sun
Down mountain roads I wander
Memories flood my aching heart
Along the way I ponder

I remember so well that September day
When you asked me to be your bride
You slipped a ring upon my hand
With tears of joy we cried

I was yours and you were mine
We promised to love each other only
But then one day God called you home
Now I walk alone and lonely

Carrie L. Reger

"in memory of my husband, Ross Reger"

As Close As My Heart

Arms aching to hold you
Lips aching to kiss you
Hands aching to touch you
If only you were here

My soul longing to be with you
My heart longing to tell you
All of its secrets
If only you were here

Love does not give a thought to distance
Nor to time as it rolls by
Only to what is in the hearts
Of those who share its magic

Separated by distance
You seem so very far
But I love you more than anything
And you will always be just as close as my heart

Grey Winds

Moth And Flame

I'm hot;
get closer.

Why not?
You know
you like the flame.

Come on in,
fly closer;
play the game.

I'm warm;
I'll be your friend.
Let the flicker of my pretty, bright flame
speed your mortal end.

For you were meant for me,
and together we have
a curious destiny.

Charles Albano

"to passionate lovers everywhere"

It's A Guy Thing

Football games
On Monday night
Buffalo wings
And Miller Lite
Fishing trips
Expensive toys
Playing poker
With the boys
One-night stands
Another notch
Always grabbing
At their crotch
Macho talk
Ego trips
Poking fun
With witty quips
Special dates
Remembered not
A birthday card
That they forgot
Hidden feelings
Deep inside
And the tears
They choose to hide
Won't admit
When they are wrong
Must always prove
They are so strong
Mid-life crisis
Thinning hair
Life is always
So unfair

With all their faults
And odd ball quirks
They really are
A bunch of jerks

    Chuck Pool

10 Rules Of Love

Love of yourself
 is where you must start.
You must love yourself
 within your own heart.

Love is a treasure
 that's worthless when hidden,
for love has no value
 until it is given.

Loving and liking
 are two different things:
You feel good when you like,
 but with love your heart sings.

Between lusting and loving,
 there should be no mistake:
In loving you give,
 in lusting you take.

Love is not something
 you withhold out of spite.
Don't use it as ammo
 when you argue or fight.

Love's not a contest
 or some kind of game.
It need not be equal,
 nor always the same.

Love's not a fire
 that consumes as it burns.

It's a path filled with life,
  as it twists and it turns.

Love is alive,
  like a plant it needs care.
Neglect it, it withers,
  its branches laid bare.

Love's spark cannot travel
  through connections amiss.
You renew each of these
  when you hug and you kiss.

Someone can love you
  and ne'er give a sign.
Be fair with your friends
  treat them gentle and kind.

    B.W. Behling

    "to Donna, whose gentle touch is love defined"

Miracle On My Patio

In a patio corner
One day last spring,
I happened upon
An amazing thing.

In a silk plant that hangs
As an afterthought,
A hummingbird found
The home she had sought.

With soft down of spiders
And skill that is blessed,
This feathery jewel
Had constructed a nest.

Patiently guarding and
Keeping it warm,
She made sure her nursery
Came to no harm.

How tireless she was
Searching for food,
Flying flower to flower
To nourish her brood.

And the awe that I felt
Goes beyond words...
To witness the first flight
Of new hummingbirds.

Sheila Cadilli

"*for nature lovers everywhere*"

Broken River Blues

.........Deep within the silence of my thoughts,
there's a special place I dream.
Down a long country road,
on the outskirts of town.
Where two hearts could meet,
with no one around.
Weeds and wild flowers, carpet the bank.
Cascading boulders, flow trickles of sand.
Like a bridge to our past,
This river of stone, holds much more.
Alone in the valley, hand in hand,
decisions were made, and promises kept.
The wind whispered passion, wild and free,
we tasted forever, and all that could be.
Only you know the words,
to the song in my heart.
We're bound by the soul,
...Till death do us part...

Butterfly Dreams

A Silent God

When you're going through some trials
The burdens are hard to bear,
You call out to God
But it seems He isn't there.

In the presence of a silent God
There's nothing you can do,
But put your faith in Jesus
And know He'll see you through.

If He answered plain and clear
Every time you called His name,
You'd never soar to heights unknown
Your faith would stay the same.

We know that it's the wings of faith
That carry us above
The lonely, hurting trials of life
To God's perfect, peaceful love.

Carrie L. Reger

Between Your House And Mine

There's a mile of lonely nights
  and a broken heart or two,
A street of sad song memories
  of the life I had with you.

There's our children who are crying,
  It happens every time
They pack their things to make the trip
  between your house and mine.

A trail of bitter tears is followed,
  The direction is unclear.
It seems we're heading from here to nowhere
  to get from there to here.

Though the road grows familiar
  with the passage of time,
That trip is still so hard to make
  between your house and mine.

Between your house and mine
  are years instead of miles,
Between your house and mine
  are tears instead of smiles.

There is more than just the distance,
  There is more than just the time
That makes the journey rough
  between your house and mine.

Martha Powell-Mitchell

Breath Of Life

I wanna run to the meadows of comfort,
Lay in the flowers of beauty,
Bathe in the warmth of God's love from the sun,
Breath the air of joy and reminisce of laughter,
Walk through the forest of imagination,
Drink from the waterfall of purity, peace and magic,
Sleep under the stars of dreams and sunsets of memories,
Wake up to the sunrise of hope,
And run to arms of eternal love.

Kelsey Blackmore

Upon Meeting

Upon meeting, a kiss!
   A glance I carried off with me
Salutation, beloved moment in bliss
   A sanctuary into which I flee
   Captive to an instant, I will miss
   But more, what may never be

   Though what is, as it is
And what is not, hear my plea!
   If I had but a single wish
The first I would think is of thee
   And upon meeting, the kiss!
   And wish you were with me

Jerry Chiccarine

Blow Me A Kiss

She blew me a kiss
From the palm of her hand
And my lips puckered up
Where I thought it would land
A sensual delight
From two luscious lips
That flowed with a passion
Off her fingertips
My heart was aflutter
Knowing soon I would get
A taste of her lust
So romantically wet
The distance between us
Was just a stone's throw
So the kiss I awaited
Had a short way to go
How long could it take
Her lips to meet mine
Moistened and colored
Like red ruby wine
The seconds ticked on
And my heart pounded so
The kiss I was yearning
Was traveling too slow
When finally it came
I was nervous and weak
And the kiss I so longed for
Landed smack on my cheek

    Bob Pool

...And He Whispered (Dual Poems)

Warm breath
and whispers

"Sweet, sweet woman...

in my ear,
waking up

...my forever darling...

more than
my mind.

...I've never been...

Love's arrows
pierce through

...so happy.

dreams, slice
through sleep fog,

I've never known...

arousing the her-parts;
soft as a sigh,

...such love.

yet as fast as
hummingbird wings.

I now know...

Once awake, raw
passion takes hold of

...the purpose of...

" " my life." "

C.J. Heck

Love Unrequited

Bringing sorrow and joy,
Pleasure and pain,
It starves yet it feeds me,
Through sunshine and rain.

It breaks my heart,
Yet makes it whole.
It weakens my body,
Yet strengthens my soul.

It empties my spirit,
Yet fills it once more.
It holds me down,
Yet lifts me to soar.

It brings me terror,
Yet comforts my fears.
It makes me cry,
Yet dries away my tears.

It leads me to loneliness,
Yet holds my hand.
It pushes me down,
Yet helps me to stand.

As I dream and I wonder,
It aches in my heart,
Yet it pulls me through life.
It's more painful to part.

Love unrequited:
A love that endures.
It stabs yet it heals me.
It hurts yet it cures.

C. Elizabeth

"*to those who have experienced the ups and downs of unrequited love.*"

The Actor

You have no way to ever tell
Who he is or where he's been
A person with no identity
No regret for any sin
He casts himself to play the part
You wish for him to be
He steals your heart and plays your mind
You are too naive to see
You play with him the perfect roles
Believing he really cares
The audience sees and knows his games
But you play along unaware
He lets you write the plot you want
And it becomes your world
But it's only all a play to him
As it is with every girl
The actor... master of illusions
An act that seems so true
He has his fun and then goes home
He won't even think of you
He thinks he holds all control
But he only holds your heart
It's something he can't understand
Because to him it's just a part
So what happens to your world
When he decides he is done
You can't imagine so much pain
Just so he could have some fun
You sit and cry and wonder why
But you'll never understand
Just know he only plays the part
For one reason... because he can.

~ *Angel* ~

"*at least it was a great show while it lasted...*"

Everytime

Kneeling down
picking up
the pieces of
my shattered heart,
like shards of
broken glass...
My eyes swollen
from the tears,
still from which
they pass...
Why did we end up
this relationship
with such a harsh shove...
It's hard to cope
with the loss of
best friends,
especially if they
were you and love.
I want so much to
talk to you when
I see you everytime...
But you don't see
the things I see
and nothing comes
from this shy
voice of mine.
I'm sorry...
so sorry...
I didn't mean to
waste your time...
It just gets harder
to pick up the pieces
from this shattered
heart of mine...
Everytime I see you...
Everytime...

Brent Clayton Faust

Do Lawd 'Member Me

Lord. I toiled dis earth so tired!
I been whipped, beaten and starved.
Plowed da fields in da rain,
When down da white man's whip came!
Runny sores all ober my body!
Sunup, sundown, I've been bent ober cotton!
Yet all my life I prayed: do I keep runnin' some mo'.....
So I stayed.

Do Lord 'member me!
Hep me da see.
Bless my spirit.
Let yo' holy ghost bekon' me.
Oh do Lord, 'member me!

John Brown stole my brotha.
Stole him to freedom Lawd!
God make him a strong leader,
And guide my brotha free
Even doe' I was caught,
Beatin,' bloodied and scarred!
But I's through runnin' Lawd!
Dis' slave may neber taste sweet freedom and joy!

Do Lawd 'member me!
Hep me da see.
Bless my spirit.
Let yo' holy ghost bekon' me.
Oh do Lawd, 'memder me!

Lawd, take me in yo' arm!
Give my sorrow'd soul
Peace and calm.
Don't firget a black slave burdin.'
Enter me in yo' purly gate.....
Fo' Jesus sake,

Do Lawd 'member me!
hep me da see.
Bless my spirit.
Let yo' holy ghost bekon' me.
Oh do Lawd 'member me!

I's tied!
I's broke down like
Da mules I plowed an werked.
I's tole I not worth dirt!
How long oh Lawd!
Fo' Jesus sake! How long!
How long.....
Do Lawd 'member me!...
'member me.

Randall Longshore

"to all the dead slaves in America"

She Happens To Be Beautiful

She smiles like the sun smiles on the clouds
She laughs like a child that laughs out loud
She cares about the little things in life
She shines like the reflection of the light
She happens to be beautiful

She smells like wildflowers dancing free
She walks through meadows and the trees
She feels the touch of life's great wonders
She cradles the lightning and the thunder
She happens to be beautiful

She clings to life's uncertainties
She knows of love's indecencies
She captures sound in a soft embrace
She sings with lips formed with grace
She happens to be beautiful...

Rod Smith

"to the love of my life"

Ransom Note

I want it all back,
Everything you have ever taken,
My heart, My hand,
the love you've foresaken.
I want my health,
my sanity, too,
I want everything
that I have ever given you.
I want my smiles,
My tears, My trust,
Give me back my kisses
if you must.
Unless these demands
are met really soon,
then I'm afraid there
will be no getting over you.

Bryana Johnson

Justice For All

He was thirty-two,
His wife was twenty-eight.
She wondered what was keeping him,
He was running very late.

Then the knock upon the door,
The cop with hat in hand.
He was speaking words to her,
She could not understand.

"I have bad news for you, my dear."
His words tore at her heart.
"Your husband was shot and killed tonight,
While pushing a grocery cart."

He had stopped to get ice cream,
For their son of three.
While there, he did more shopping,
For his precious family.

The gunman came and robbed the store,
He took the lives of three.
Her husband was among the dead,
These parting words, said he:

"Tell my wife I love her,
And my darling baby too.
Tell them I'll be watching over them,
In everything they do."

The years went by,
And life was tough.
She did the very best she could,
But things were always rough.

Finally, the date was set,
The killer was going to die.
All of us who knew them,
Could not help but wonder why.

This evil man who had wrecked their life,
Had been treated like a king.
While being cared for by the state,
You could even hear him sing.

But mom and son had carried on,
No song was in their heart.
The sadness written in their eyes,
While looking for a new start.

Now the time has come,
Tonight he was going to die.
They asked him for his menu,
What he ordered would make a statue cry.

"I'll have lobster, steak, and salad,
A piece of apple pie.
A dish of chocolate ice cream,
To cool me when I fry."

There was no lobster, steak, and salad,
For the family now of two.
Beans and fried potatoes,
Was the best that they could do.

Where is the justice in this world,
For something like this to be?
I wish that we could wake up,
Oh, why can't people see?

Why do criminals have more rights,
Than people like you and me?
We work and pay our taxes,
While they live on us for free.

Grace Martino

"to the victims of crime everywhere"

Powerful Love

Forever and always,
My love for you will be.
You will never know dear,
How much you mean to me.

I love you with all my heart,
Yet that doesn't feel quite enough.
To find the words to tell you,
I'm afraid would be too tough.

I would swim the deepest ocean,
Or climb the highest hill.
Would those statements spoken
Tell you my love is real.

Or do I quietly stand by you,
And whisper love sonnets through the day.
Will you see the love in my eyes,
While by your side I lay.

So you see I have a problem,
Coming up with a way to say.
That more than anything in this world,
I love you and will for always.

Never in all of history,
Has one loved another as much.
As the love I feel for you dear,
Our hearts and souls have touched.

Pauline Hamblin

"to all of my family and friends. Thanks for supporting me!"

The Rose

Standing in the ocean's mist
A wilted rose clutched in her fist
Thorns they pierce her tender skin
But the tears they stem from deep within

The waves come crashing to the shore
She is lost in thoughts of a time before
For so long she had kept them away
But something had awakened them this day

The rose from his casket she'd slipped
Now with her own blood it dripped
Withered by time and circumstance
Deeper she wades lost in trance

She feels the ache of a forgotten pain
How can she bear to feel it again
Her love, and the life they had conceived
Two lives lost, one left to grieve

One by one they were ripped away
Leaving her lost, searching for a way
The icy waters lap her fingertips
But never once does she loosen her grip

Feeling deserving of this guilt
That she remained after so much blood was spilt
And yet she found the strength to survive
Slowly escaping the haunting cries

Her young heart soon mended
To her new life she tended
The years... so many since she laid them to rest
So what now puts her heart to this test

Surrounded in the swirling sea
She yearns only to be free
Deep in her heart she knows
She must release the guilt with the rose.

Tammy S. Hoover

Picnic For Two

Spreading out the blanket
underneath a big shade tree
We open up the basket
that was made for you and me

There's cheese and crackers
along with a bottle of champagne
We're celebrating our love
and all that we have gained

From the very beginning
it was love at first sight
Remember seeing the stars
on that clear and glorious night?

It's almost as if they were dancing
there wasn't a cloud in the sky
The birds were softly singing
the sweetest lullaby

We'll mark our anniversary
and each dream that has come true
Every year we'll make it special
with a " Picnic for Two "

__Brenda Mae__

My Little Guy

My little guy...

My little guy is suffering,
his grades are going down,
because of all the teasing
and constant fooling around.

The other kids are on his back
because they know he's meek.
They always take advantage
and make him feel so weak.

They all gang up on him
and tease and make him cry
because they all know
that he's the one so shy.

This story is not only about
one boy who stands alone,
but about countless others, too,
that are not allowed to grow.

Dear God let me find a way
to help my little man out,
to pull him out of his rut,
a situation he can do without.

Robert L. Macchia

In My Hand

Let me take your hand in my hand
to place against my heart
to rest my cheek upon it
to kiss with lips apart.

Let me trace each digit on it
from base to slender end
out onto each painted tip
then slowly back again.

Let me take your face in my hand
to place against my heart
to rest my cheek upon it
to kiss with lips apart.

Let me trace each line on it
from brow to slender chin
out onto each rounded tip
then slowly back again.

Let me take your body in my hand
to place against my heart
to rest my cheek upon it
to kiss with lips apart.

Let me trace each tress on it
from top to every bend
out onto each reaching tip
then slowly back again.

Let me take your life in my hand
to place against my heart
to rest my cheek upon it
to kiss with lips apart.

Let me trace each day on it
from now 'til grave to tend
out onto each flower tip
then slowly back again.

Tony Spivey

Just Three Words

Just three words,
I want to hear.
Hold me close,
And touch me dear.
Shout it to the world,
Whisper in my ear.

Just three words,
I want to hear...

    Butterfly Dreams

Nature's Masterpiece

A brush of shadows
dark on light
paints a palette
of such delight...

patterns etching
here and there
scallop-edging
frills so fair...

to frame a sky
of pale azure
and mountains of
a deeper hue...

through wisps of lace
the sunbeams smile
showering silver
to beguile...

until the night
in creeping gait
deepens darkness
that cannot wait...

the scene awashed
with colorless ease
to blend and melt
nature's masterpiece...

Lydia Castilho

Shadow Song

Last night I waited patiently
for my shadow to come home
he never came, he never called
he left me there alone

In other times he's stood me up
or left me in the rain
I think he's cold, I think he's rude
He thinks I am insane

I tried to get my hands on him
he slipped away again
I don't know why I keep him near
he's a fair weather friend.

Jim Morton

Chalice Of Love

Chalice Of Love
If I say I love you
will you be mine forever
stronger than snowy peaks
warmer than Sahara sands
shimmering in silver moonlight,
will our days harmonize with
night's serenading ecstasies
moaned by infinite lovers,
will you give me yourself
each passing hour,
self-assured
confused
together
apart
in solitude
or cloistered with angels?

wintersong

Soul's Reward

In the distance music plays, a haunting melody
asking how the things that are
are really meant to be.
Fate awaits at heaven's gates
into the vast unknown,
the lot is cast
your time is past
and now you're on your own.
Promises kept, although you wept
you kept them, every one;
Never let go, and now you know
a new life has begun.

Renée Rose

"may all who dream of eternal love, find it..."

Moonlight

Will you look with eyes of sadness
If our love grows cold
Moonlight meets the dying embers
Softly shining gold

Silver glimmers on the water
Blackness in my eyes
Crackles of the dying fire
Agonizing cries

The more I talk, the less you listen
I wonder who you love
Many questions only asked
To moonlight from above

Do you see the dying embers
Of a love grown cold
Do you look with eyes of sadness
Softly shining gold

~ *Angel* ~

"for everyone who has ever had a flame die out..."

IF

If hate were love and war were peace
  what would this world be like?
Would heaven gaze upon this land
  with sunshine in her eyes?
Would God's almighty voice rejoice
  in music never heard?
And we the people would thus see
  how mankind really lived?

If man calls himself civilized
  how civilized can primitivity be?
How can machines create with love
  that which human hands once sought?
How dare man even think the thought
  his works compare with those of God's!
Why would a scientist care to raise
  a child outside its mother's womb?
I blush in shame to know I too
  am part of this mankind!

Basi Hummel

"from my youth"

Charmed

To feel his warm touch
    become drunk from his smile
No distance is too much
    I'd travel thousands of miles
To be held in his arms
    such strong loving care
To be taken in by his charms
    yet completely aware

Brenda Swanberg

Just One Kiss

Looking back through the years
   To all my dreams, hopes, and fears
I see her there, along the way
   Waiting for this fateful day

What we had, I could not see,
   My eyes were closed, my mind not free
If there was love, it did not show
   In my heart, I did not know

But in the dark, all of this
   Came to light, with just one kiss
A kiss so sweet, filled with desire
   Touched my lips, and felt like fire

What happens now is up to us
   Forever waits, there is no rush
So as we grow, side by side
   Love is out, no more to hide

   Michael J. Tripp

     "to my beautiful Brenda"

My Little Sister

Let me tell you about my Father,
Let me tell you about my Mother.
They only had two children,
A sister and a brother.

But Father has passed away now,
Mother also went one day.
That just left me and sister,
And we went our separate way.

Twenty years I chose the Air Force,
I never did get home.
California for my sister,
We both were meant to roam.

With letters and with pictures,
We always kept in touch.
Missing growing up together
And things that meant so much.

Maybe writing down this poem
In my own and simple way,
Will tell her about my feelings,
I never got to say.

But how do you put on paper
all the ways you've really missed her,
Of all the time that's passed away
without your little sister?

From in my heart, I found this poem
And hope she knows it's true...
With all my love in five small words:
Sister, Sandi, I love you.

Bob Brokaw

The Tree In My Own Backyard

I come from blood not Rich nor Poor
the middle class, not need much more.
A Family;
   That of Genuine Strength,
    a Bourgeois Tree of such length.
And mighty are those ancient roots,
never to bark such prejudice suits,
for wisdom grew from deep within,
a tradition laid down by fellow kin.

And although a branch
weak and ill,
I shall carry the strength and family will
and bound towards tradition
hence...

   I may die,
   but my tree shall live,
   flourish,
   with much love to give,
   and wisdom,
   a treasure fold,
   my Tree,
   shall stand so bold.

...brings life to my tree such radiance!

   John Dee

Finding Hope

can you find what you really lost
or is it all just in your head
do you think that dreams are real
or do you think they're dead

do you hope for what tomorrow brings
and do you think it's good
can you see your life right now
and is it like it should

can you find the future
in the eyes of your reflection
what is it that you hope for
in your thoughts and contemplation

do you hope for friendship
or do you hope for love
can you find it on the earth
or in the heavens up above

search for what you hope is true
and hope that it is all there
find a love inside of you
and hope that it is fair

Dave Nieman

"for all those people who think they have lost hope."

What We Leave Behind

Late one night an angel came to me
And told me that my time was up
And that I must look back on my life
To see all I had done

I saw my childhood, my first steps, my first words
My first day of school as well
I saw all the love I had been given
For this was easy to tell

I saw my first car, and my graduation day
I saw my first day of college come and go
And my last day as well, just as quickly
I wanted to see no more

I saw my marriage, and I saw it fall apart
I saw business meetings galore
I saw my fancy cars and my big house
But I saw no happiness before

I saw money beyond my dreams
I saw possessions, parties and fame
While my children grew without their father
I would never be the same

The images disappeared and the angel said
'What do you have to show?'
And I broke down and cried like a baby
For I had everything in the world, but nothing worthwhile to show

It is clear, the angel said.
You did not understand
The meaning behind this gift called life
Given to every man

For life is not what you can gain
But rather what you can give
To find joy in each day, each moment
For true happiness lies within

I wasted my life, I cried
In my rush for worldly things
I did not live to seize each day
Nor all the joy it brings

I awoke the next morn alive and quite well
My life forever changed
I vowed to seize every moment of every day
See the sunshine behind the rain

But what will be your legacy
When your days on earth are through
Will you leave behind joyful days
Or will you waste your days, too

To make a difference in someone's life
To love with all of your soul
These are life's hidden treasures
These will make you whole

So rush about in your life if you must
And I only pray that you'll find
That how we live is far more important
Than what we leave behind

Grey Winds

...Well, You Know

I'm remembering your warm brown eyes
The smile you could not disguise
There are times I miss your sigh
How does always mean good-bye

The path is narrow, the road is long
Please darling, try to be strong
With you is where I belong
How can this love be so wrong

You are distant now--I feel the space
Wish I wasn't easy to replace
Will you think of me--my face
Will time all of me erase

You are the heart of all I am
And the breath that begins my day
I can't think of you as a friend
And there are times I want to say
That I still... well, you know
Please don't let me go

D. L. Frantz

"For my DAF... well, you know why, and to Bernie for comfirming beliefs."

Keep To Your Heart

Little Angel deep tears that cry
don't let such haste wave your love good-bye
for on that day when your love comes to you
it will have true meaning and honesty too
so trust in your faith and never let go
and keep dear to your heart the one you love so.

John Dee

The Necklace

I wear a special necklace
  its little links are gold
you gave it for my birthday
  when I was feeling old

On the chain there is a heart
  a little rose inlay
That always makes me think of you
  each and ev'ry day

This necklace is so special
  it's the last thing that you gave
Before you went to heaven, and
  the last thing that I saved

The necklace will remain
  a symbol of my love
to you, my son, who left this world
  to go to be above

And tho' I do not understand
  why you had to go
I know there was a better plan
  'though what, I do not know

But someday we will meet again
  our faces shining bright
Because we'll meet in heaven
  within the heavenly light

so until that day, my first born son
  that's the way it'll be
You'll always be that inlaid rose
  within the heart of me

Dhynah

"in memory of my son who died of cancer in 1994"

Dreamin' ~

i'm lost in my dreams again
    as your tongue encircles mine
my heart~ beating uncontrollably
    i've lost all sense of time
i'm a prisoner of emotion
    within your warm embrace
but i'll gladly give up freedom
    hell, i'd move to outer space
if i could be there with you, right now
    and feel your love inside
i'd give up all earthly possessions
    and you could take away my pride
'cause there's nothin' that i need~ but you
    no, no one could compete
your kisses bring me home again
    i've never tasted anything so sweet
so, i'll be your lil angel
    and i'll be your naughty girl
i'll give you what you never had
    take you to another world
'cause you make me go so crazy
    hot whispers in my ear
i swear i've been to heaven
    each time you hold me near...

Kathleen Kerry Swanson

Sunrise

the sun rises, shining light on a dark world
shades of pink and orange fill the sky
as light chases away the shadows
the flowers open up to show their brilliant colors
the clouds part to reveal a clear blue sky
as the sun rises, a new day begins
a new day full of discoveries
a new day full of dreams
a new day to accomplish goals
a new day for a second chance
a new day bringing hope

Sunny Pierce

Forever & A Day

I want to love you
give you all that you desire
I want to share with you
all the happiness you inspire
I want to hold your hand
every moment that remains
I want to see your face
forever as I awake
I want to hear your voice
always call my name
I want to love you
forever and a day.

Tammy Lively-Sellers

"to the love of my life, Gary Peterman"

A Picnic With Shakespeare

Wandering through fields of green,
the forest was painted a majestic scene.
My vision focused and eyesight keen,
strolling through a midsummer's night dream.

With my Juliet shaded with oak,
her silken hair I begin to stroke,
Anticipation high, full of hope.

But as was Shakespeare, too poor for college,
perhaps I'll finish this poem
when I acquire more knowledge.

Christopher A. Smith

Another Time, Another Place

Before sleep arrives
I often think of you
Your smile,
Your soft brown eyes
How tender, yet strong
A hug can feel
All you've said
All you've done
You've touched my heart
And captured my soul
I cherish each moment
As if it were our last
I grasp each word
As if it were final
A simultaneous beginning
To an infinite ending
I ache for a touch
A hand to hold
This space is empty
My heart is full
So much love
And none to taste
Another time…
Another place

D. L. Frantz

I Sometimes Think Dark Thoughts

In this cold, dark place
I sometimes come to think
About some things. Things
Like Why am I here?
And Why do I still want to live?

As I look at myself through
Darkest green orbs of darkness
And light, I wonder about
Myself, my mind, my life, and
What I am worth.

Why should I stay? I cry
To myself in this cold, dark
Place I seem to come to
Whenever I feel I am
Worthless, and don't want to live.

But then the sun comes out,
And my spirit brightens, along
With this cold, dark place. It
Transforms into a bright, blue
Place, transfiguring my deep, dark thoughts.

Now I can say, Why did I
Think that? And knowing that
I should stay on this earth,
If only to protect the ones I love
From ever thinking these deep, dark thoughts.

Amanda Piotrowski

Always Daddy's Girl

Last night while you were sleeping,
Daddy crept quietly into your room.
I sat beside you, sweetheart,
And said, My girl... you grew up too soon.
It seems like only yesterday
When you played with Barbie Dolls,
When you ran down Main Street
Bouncing rubber balls.
How I long for those yesterdays
When you were my baby girl.
You used to ask for simple candy,
And now you ask for diamonds and pearls.
You grew out of size four sneakers,
And now you wear high heels.
You never cared for fancy clothes,
These days, it seems like a big deal.
Your hair was fine in pigtails
When you were eight or nine.
Now you make sure every hair's in place,
And today, you comb it all the time.
Yes, you're no longer Daddy's Baby,
You look all grown up to me.
You're so beautiful, my precious,
Honey, that is so plain to see.
Soon you'll find a special man
Who will steal your heart away,
And Daddy misses you already
As I look at you today.
Good-bye, my little baby,
Sleep tight, my little Pearl,
Always remember that in my heart,
You're Daddy's Little Girl.

Andrea L. Michano

"*to my dad, Roy, and all daddy's girls out there!*"

Mirror

Mirrors

If I told you
how beautiful you are
would you believe me?
Would you trust the image
glowing on my face
or would you hide
in shadows
cast by sunless worlds?

And if I told you
all the beauty you behold
is what you feel,
radiating,
would you believe the mirror
in my eyes
or would you hide
within the shadows
of your heart.

wintersong

When Love Could Be So Easy

When love could be so easy
When life could be so grand
When trust should be so simple
For a woman and a man

And souls should lock together
In a union of the heart
And never let another
Try and tempt the two apart

So in the darkest hours
When thoughts are filled with doubt
And words are shot like arrows
And blame is tossed about

When thoughts are lost in sorrow
Self-pity and self-doubt
We always have the power
To sort the whole thing out

For you and I are lovers
Together, make our stand
'Cause love can be so easy
And life can be so grand.

Jim Morton

First Kiss

It lingers still
the thrill
that sent a chill
up and down
all over me
when first
your lips
did tenderly,
kiss.

Dale Edmands

"for Leslie"

Another Ride?

I am on a roller coaster
  on another ride
First it was the merry-go-round
  so what's next? a slide?

My life is like a carnival
  fun until it rains
Then I run for cover
  then back to playing games

This roller coaster's not much fun
  it makes my tummy queasy
But I guess that it's all right
  cuz life is never easy

With all the ups and downs,
  the going fast and slow
It really makes me wonder
  what is the "main show"

How long is the main event
  and do I have to stay
Until the tents are packed and closed
  'til I can go away?

Well I guess I'll stick around
  to see what happens next
You never know, what's round the bend
  just maybe I'll be blessed

    Dhynah

Artist

The colors
from your soul,
collect and bring
this man to life.
Paint me with blue...
paint me with red...
paint with any feeling
you choose...
I'll always be here
on your canvas
My outline still
jagged but loose....
You are my artist,
you complete my smile.
You bring to life
a sense in me...
Something I lost
when I was a child.
Swirl with color,
the warmth and glow
the feelings you've
always kept...
Blend the shadows
bring the light...
Let my paint dry
and set...
Take me and show me...
let the world know,
you took me from nothing
painted me tenderly
ever so...

You are my artist
you complete my life
caressing my features
with your palette
and knife...
Wishing I could be
your real love...
If only paintings
could come to life...

Brent Clayton Faust

"to my best friends Leah Frerichs, Melissa Husk, and Amanda Larson"

Hard Drive

for months I've partitioned - sectored my strife
trying to determine - wrong from the right
clinging to bits - healing the bytes
moving and changing – formatting new life

my career crashed - with it my dreams
memory erased – circuits burned clean
connection to love – garbled and crossed
power was fading – all color was lost

a new system needed – more power and thrill
new creativity – speed and the skill
designing new backup – restoring my line
application of will – turn tables on time

tap my known current – discarding old woes
erase obsolete system – vanquish all foes
move to the center – empower self trust
stun all the comers – lightning fast thrust

no longer lay down – and wait for the call
stand up and fight – pin them to the wall
knowing I'm better – than any machine
time to arise – from a protracted dream

and so I forgo – all advise of claimed best
listen inside – put myself to the test
it's hard but I'm winning – getting better by day
pain is less troubling – I'll continue this way

    The Poet Who Lies Within

Jim Culhane

Rain

rain
1/8/99
7:14 p.m.

Cold, alone
dark and howling wind
rustling leaves and shifting spirits
rain pitter-pattering
puddles forming
memories swimming
and to think you're not here.
funny how this winter night
reminds me so much of you
dressed in gloves
scarf in hand
the sound of thunder
laughter ringing
teardrops falling
I am falling
deeper, quicker
please don't stop me
don't let this love slow down
lazy summers
hasty winters
everything reminds me of you
and I'm lonely
yet I'm smiling
thoughts still spinning
you in red
you before me
you with hands around my shoulders

holding me
taking me
tasting me
telling me that everything will be okay
that you are mine and I am yours
kissing me
loving me
having me
telling me the rain will end
but it's falling like I'm falling
and you stand before me
with your gentle smile
and rain and wind
and thunder lightning
don't seem to matter anymore
and I hug you
and I kiss you
with my closed eyes
and my open heart.

J.C. Monterrosa

Love Is

Love is the tingle that makes me feel right,
And all the gentle hugs felt through the night.
Love is the feeling that nothing shall harm,
And the goose pimply feeling as you rub my arm.
Love is the kiss that ignites in me a fire,
Filling my soul with passion and pleasant desire.
Love is the heart that pounds in my chest,
As you pay attention to me and none of the rest.

Anthony Limes

Ode To A Cheeseburger

How do I eat thee
Let me salivate the ways

With cheese so creamy
My mind blurs to a haze

Lettuce and maters so fresh and crisp
I savor each moment plunged through my lips

A patty so full of animal fat
I tend to forget even where I am at

As your ketchup and mustard run down my chin
I know I must bite again and again

Within your bun all covered with sesame
I feel your power has got the best of me

I try and try with all my might
But with a swig of beer you're out of sight

I spy on a platter so close sits your brother
As I feared, the same fate he will suffer

Suffer and suffer though he may
I shall live to gobble another day.

Christopher A. Smith

"to Sherry and all lovers of animal fat"

Trusted Love

Love is on the way,
I can see the signs,
I am ever seeking you,
You are always on my mind.

We are two peas in a pod,
You're my soul mate and friend,
Together we'll be for always,
Our love, knows no end.

Unselfish, trusted love,
An arrow of cupid's true,
Many are the reasons,
That I fell in love with you.

More than all the world could give,
And more than this poet could say,
I grow more in love with you,
Each and every day.

Max The Poet©

"to the lady who is my everything... I Love You"

To Say Good-bye To You

The sun was always shining
The skies were always blue
It was so easy back then
To fall in love with you.

You held the gift of promise
A key to open my soul
Never had I felt so complete
Your love made me whole.

When I walked into a room
I saw the twinkle in your eyes
Your face told a thousand stories
For you, there was no disguise.

You loved me so simple
Without ever asking for any more
Than what I was, who I would be
I know you never shared your heart before.

Every minute, every second
I wanted to be in your embrace
All your happiness, all your love
Showed upon your face.

Every love song in the universe
Every poem that is true
Every star in this galaxy
Was meant for me and you.

Not even for a moment
Did I doubt your honesty

I always knew, inside my heart
This is how love was supposed to be.

And I'm sorry for not showing you
On each and every day
All the things your love made me feel
In each and every way.

And I'm so sorry for hurting you
By taking you for granted
Believe me, when I say
You're the man I've always wanted.

I could go on a million years
For an eternity or two
But instead, I'll end and only hope
Happiness, joy, and contentment for you.

The sun no longer shines as bright
The skies are not as blue
And I find it the most difficult thing
To say goodbye to you...

Kathleen Kerry Swanson

"to Mom, Dad, Barry, and the love of my life"

Silent

Hush my sweet darling
    Don't say a word, let it be
Love is best~ silent

Kathleen Kerry Swanson

Old-Fashioned Guy

I'm not into health food.
I'm a steak and potatoes man.
I'm not into tofu,
just plain old raisin bran.
I'm not into business cards,
though I work hard with a smile.
I'm not into designer clothes,
I'd rather create my own style.
I'm not so much into myself
to keep my head up in the sky.
I like me just the way I am.
I'm just an old-fashioned guy.

Can't keep up with expensive trends
and there's no reason to try.
No change in habits, or change of friends,
I'm just an old-fashioned guy.

I'm into commitments.
Promises don't bother me.
I'll feel no resentments.
I got no time for cheap vanity.
I'm not into money,
but I got my piece of the pie.
Dollar bill ain't everything
to an old-fashioned guy.

Don't want any seasonal friends,
for company I have to buy.
Don't need colored contacts lens.
I'm just an old-fashioned guy.

I'm into true loving.
Romantic ties don't frighten me.
I'm into soft moonlight,
sweet music and slow melodies.
I'm into long romance,
with sparkling stars up in the sky.
Simplicity means everything
to an old-fashioned guy.

Amun-Ra

"to the 'real' people"

The Agony In A Teardrop

The silence of a teardrop
screams out in tormented pain.

The flood of many teardrops
is like a torrential rain.

They'll drown a broken heart
or suffocate a tender soul.

They'll flow without compassion
when they're on a roll.

They roll down hill so easily
and it's hard to make them stop.

But stop they must
when there isn't...
any more to drop.

T. J. Daniels

Walk With Me To The Shoreline

the calm before the storm
bids us to ignore the brewing tempest
still the nimbus are towering beyond the horizon
as inexorably the squall line approaches our respite

walk with me to the shoreline
for I fear not the fury
stand with me to confront the shifting currents
and prevail the harsh elements before us
as the laden columns rise to blot the sky
and seize the light from our tomorrow
I shall rise up in contest
to ensure the continuance of our day

with a fury for the typhoon
its winds will not deter me our days
the surf will pound around us
and violent gusts will tear at our fabric
but I refuse to be swept up in these tides
just as these winds will dwindle to zephyrs before me
the lightning will strike and the thunder echo
but they shall gather not my attention
for I focus on the quieter seas to follow
in the days of lesser tumult
when the gentle breeze but wisps your hair
and the setting sun casts us in pleasant repose

I have seen these days before
and desire the grace of their twilight to come
they surpass any fury which can be leveled
and make as nothing the monsoon

so for now I await the storm with you here
when it arrives I shall raise my shield
to protect you from its vengeance
while we may become dampened
we shall not drown
while we may be shaken by thunder
we shall not be disheartened
and as the seas rise around us
our determination will summon its eye

in the morning the sun will rise again
casting its view over the remnants
in these we will find that which we ever needed
the distractions will be blown from us
and we will sail the seas of our life
collecting the cherished
leaving the deadweight behind

here in this calm before the coming storm
walk with me to the shoreline
trust me to shelter you
I'll keep you ever sound
and in allowing me this protection
you shall shelter me

        The Poet Who Lies Within

Jim Culhane

    "to Susan"

My Travels

My life has been a long road,
I've walked it day by day.
There's been a lot of detours,
and many tolls to pay.

I've walked Wisconsin waters,
open spaces of the West.
Around the world and back again,
have put me to the test.

I spent some time in England,
ate crumpets, fish, and tea.
That's where I met my first wife,
who's no longer here with me.

No time to raise three children,
a family was too slow.
No room for them in traveling,
for a man who's on the go.

Vietnam, another story...
best leave these things unsaid.
The sights of crying children,
their world of living dead.

Friends were left behind me,
no longer to be found.
Another chain to bind me,
from my travels all around.

A road without direction,
no map to show the way.
Just travel it forever,
and take it day by day.

The nights which brought the darkness,
lost loves, hopes, and fears.
The rain that fell at daybreak,
was caused by a thousand tears.

With all these miles behind me,
and nothing left to see.
I never found the person,
I hoped and dreamed to be.

A home with forty acres,
a wife to share your day.
I never stopped to find it,
it passed along the way.

If I were now a tour guide,
and your trip you ask I plan.
I'd show the world beside you,
reach out and take it's hand.

Don't ask for distant pleasures,
and all the things I've tried.
Take the time to really love life,
with a friend there by your side.

So many things are missing,
if you rush your life away.
So slow your pace a little,
as you live it day by day.

Don't leave a loving family,
for things you think you lack.
For when you really miss them,
no road will take you back.

Don't end up forever going,
like me alone to roam.
Searching, searching, searching,
for a road to take you home.

For when the road has ended,
too late your life to save.
You'll see the final signpost.
"5 miles ahead to grave".

    Bob Brokaw

Just As I Think

Just as I think, there's no hope in sight
Something always happens, that makes me feel right.
Just as I think, there's no hope around
God gives me the thing, which picks me up from the ground.
Just as I think, I've been totally forsaken
Something always happens, and I know I'm mistaken.
Just as I think, I'm not worth a dime
Something always happens, almost all of the time.
Just as I think, my life is a total mess
God helps me to see others, and mine's not so bad; I must confess.
Just as I think, I might know it all
God gives me the chance, to slip down and fall.

Anthony Limes

Casting Stones

I look to blame anyone else
For bringing me here, to pain and dread.
Cold and sharp, these stones in my hand,
I draw back my fist and aim straight for your head.
I hesitate for just a moment.
Do I really wish you harm?
My fingers clenched round cruel, sharp edges,
Warm blood running down my arm.
How can I cast the first stone?
The guilt and blame are mine as well.
And how many more must follow it
To ward away my private Hell?
What can be gained by casting stones,
By bringing you down in a vengeful attack?
It can't change the past, it can't ease the pain,
And I can't move forward if I must look back.

Julia Warfel

Unspoken Words

I should have told you darling...
That I love you
Should have made it very clear
My unspoken was so true
Now I'm wishing you were here
If I could do it all over
And turn back the hands of time
I would tell you that I love you
And that I'm grateful that you're mine
I always thought it was something that I said
But it was unspoken...
unspoken words instead

Maurice Sherry

"to Liz and Sue of VAHS Buffalo, thanks!"

I'm A Guy

I dig the way you look at me, when I pose you sigh
I know I deserve that look, after all I'm a guy
When I eat my food too fast and you wonder why
It's so I can taste it each time I belch, yep, I'm a guy
When I love you a certain way, and you moan, oh my!
I think I'm the first to touch you like that, 'cause, I'm a guy
When you dress so sexy, I think I'll love you 'til I die
You know the reason, don't ya, you're a girl, I'm a guy

John Henry Scott

"Jan, you inspired me to write again... thank you!"

I.M.i.s.s.Y.o.u.

In the late night hours, the

Morning seems to come sneaking
in to
see if I am
still okay... and

You know you're the
only one I love... I
understand, we can't be together... but... I miss you!

Odessa Lynette Price

"MM, I love and miss you!"

Storms On The Ocean

Mama, don't cry for me.
I know in the end it will be alright.
Please do not cry for me.
I know in the end we will always find light.
Don't waste your tears on me.
We've walked through the lightning and flood
in the past.
And you've always been there with me.
And we've built a love that will always last.
When the road turned dark and cold,
I've always known there was a hand I could hold.

It's just another storm on the ocean.
The rain is falling hard today,
But we have seen storms on the ocean,
And so far they never have blown us away.
We've stood through the raging wind
Because we knew when we had to bend.
It may be raging tonight,
But the dawn will bring light,
After this storm on the ocean.

I know we'll make it through.
Some storms have been too painful to mention.
At the very worst moments I knew
We were fighting the fears of our own invention.
We know what we have to do
When outside the hurricane screams.
We have to remember what's true.
We can't let these storms wash away all our dreams.
When I just want to run away,
You have been my reason to stay.

So it's just another storm on the ocean.
The rain is falling hard today,
But we have seen storms on the ocean,
And so far they never have blown us away.
We've stood through the raging wind
Because we knew when we had to bend.
It may be raging tonight,
But the dawn will bring light,
After this storm on the ocean.

Julia Warfel

"to my wonderful mother"

He Let Me Hold His Hand

Last night we filled his tote bag up
and laid out his new clothes.
Talking about the day ahead,
I watched his excitement grow.

He asked Jesus to be with him
as he faced the coming day,
and later on, while on my knees,
I had to do the same.

The morning light came quickly
this rite of passage now at hand,
and I'm forced to see the face
of Momma's little man.
He smiles as he dresses,
and readily agrees
that kindergarten will be so much fun,
and he can't wait to see.

Walking to school must seem like miles
to a little boy of five,
both mother and child trying to fight
the trepidation growing inside.
Impending changes in our lives,
I'm sure he doesn't understand,
but I know he's still my baby,
because he let me hold his hand.

Paula Duquette

Poet To Poet

Writing in verse
The two of us
Combining our thoughts
Making love with words
Creating lines that flow
That capture the reader's heart
Sharing our deepest feelings
Standing naked before the world
Knowing it's worth the risk
To touch another's soul
We pour out ourselves
Fulfilling an inner need
As we carefully pen each word
I sit in awe as I wait for your words
Captivated by what I have already seen
My own words... beginning to form
From the depths of my subconscience
Ready to erupt from within
It seems sometimes we are reading each other's minds
Our thoughts co-joined somehow
Each time we meet
I feel a closer bond
Sharing more of myself in my words
As we unite our creative spirits
And explore each other's minds
Living out our dreams... our fantasies...
For those who dare to read...

Sandra Wommack

Exile

Sin from thine eyes, wished
Cast upon thee
Slumber divine, I awake for you only.
Fairest you are, youthful
Gallant star
That lies in my sky
Subdue to few, you shine
And catch my eye.
Dear lover, I call thee;
Why does thou not reply?
Coy little boy, spindle upon
My finger
Does prick and stay much to linger.
Watch me and listen to my word
Herald upon you now... BE MINE!
Yet, thou does not come hence...

She calls, and what shall I do?
Be front on your reality, or throw
Emotion askew.
Frank, dear lady,
I love you not more
Yet, I hesitate to burn you
And leave much you adore.
Conceive oh mistress,
My devotion is true
But to some other bounty
A love is mine; not you.
Gracious and flattered
And praise heard to be,
Engage not too fondly;
Say not to love ME.
Amorous fatigue,
Curse brought by thine eye
Take to course, lovely lady,
Adoration PLEASE to shy.

Oh heaven! Don't deceive!
Make these blind eyes see!
Speak kind words my love!
Tell how you love no one but me!
Disappoint me not, for I feel like a
Stupid fop!
So sure was my beauty and sweet charm.
You do this anguish heart great harm.
Standing in shadows I gaze at you.
I gaze at her. Were you and
She meant to be?
I'll stab my heart a thousand times,
For the thousand times
I wished you mine!...
You wished you mine!!

Oh Son of God who dwells so far.
If by some way I knew to comfort her!
She was like a lovely day in May!
If only my heart was not taken!
Now God's mercy takes her far away,
And I feel the worst!
My heart and soul have been
Dragged through dirt!

Randall Longshore & Elyse Ford

Cold Champagne Dreams

Much as an artist
treasures his oils,
she holds tight to
her cold champagne dreams.
Dreams that warm on
the coldest of nights
from a time
nothing else has replaced.
She savors the moments
locked tightly away
for only the night
holds the key
to unleash the memories
she buries inside
while marking time
in a warm beer life.
Those cold champagne dreams
of red roses and love,
its moments spent
safe in his arms
where the tenderest kiss
she still felt
on her breast
even now
this many years past.
Weeping eyes shut tight
as a clam in the sea
she now pleads
no more memories tonight.

For nothing is worse
to a woman like this,
her deep passion
lies dying inside,
only allowing the want
the incredible need
to bubble up in
her cold champagne dreams.

C.J. Heck

In Love With You

All day, my heart soars!
Look, I can touch the sky,
kiss the sun, draw images
of you in each passing
cloud- I am weightless,
free-flying!
Catch the glimmer
on my wings;
smiles for every
thought of you!

Dale A. Edmands

"for Elainie"

So In Love With You

Light up the fire, open some wine
where does the time go, it's quarter 'til nine
I can't believe that you're finally mine
I'm so in love with you

Once on a weekend, in April or May
I wasn't sure I'd convinced you to stay
what would I do if you left me today
I'm so in love with you

    Reeling,
      feeling,
swimming in my soul.
    Ocean,
      motion,
finally feeling whole.

If you were wondering, let me insist
yours are the tastiest lips that I've kissed
when you're around I can barely resist
I'm so in love with you

    Either,
      neither,
anything we choose.
    slower,
      lower,
honey, we can't lose.

Snuggle up closer and show me a sign
I know the naughtiest way to unwind
turn out the lights and who knows what we'll find
I'm so in love with you...
    and you know how it's true....

Jim Morton

We Kissed With Nature

we danced on a sandy shore
we sang such a pretty tune
we traded smiles galore
while we made love with the moon

we played in the sunlit rays
we wrestled with our dreams
we spoke of everlasting days
while we made love in a stream

we teased cloudy skies so sweet
we chased a rainbow's pot of gold
we ran naked down a rainy street
while we made love with the cold

we dashed across open meadows
we picked the freshest flowers
we comforted each from the shadows
while we made love for hours

we kissed with nature...

spring we spent with open arms
while flowers craved to bloom
fall we flew with kites on air
while leaves fell to their doom
winter we played with snowy hills
while skies remained so blue
summer we played in ocean waves
while the horizon showed its view
we kissed with nature...

Rod Smith

"for S.S., with love..."

A Butterfly

That morning
you left me,
a strangely colored,
but beautiful butterfly
caught its wing
in my front door.
It put up a struggle
so intense,
I had forgotten
my own loss
in watching it.

This morning
as you lie beside me,
I replay the words
you said to me.
You truly wanted your freedom,
but something held on to you
tightly enough
to make you stay.

Yesterday
I saw another butterfly.
It wasn't the same one.
The other one died
on my front porch.

Paula Duquette

Live On (Peter's Poem)

Love could not hold you,
Nor could our tears.
You suffered in silence,
Enslaved by your fears.
Now mortal boundaries,
Keep us apart,
But live in my memory...
Live on in my heart.

Julia Warfel

"in memory of Peter Towner"

Describing Heaven

All of my friends ask about
The woman who stole my heart
Describing you is difficult
Because we live so far apart

I speak of your beauty
And the way you smile
As I start to picture you
It shortens every mile

I tell them of your hair
Moving as you walk
And how every time you look at me
I find it hard to talk

I mention how your eyes
Keep me in a trance
Oh, to see those eyes again
I'll jump at every chance

I cannot describe all of you
I can barely scrape the top
Because describing heaven
Is harder than I thought.

Danny Grubb

"to someone very special to me who lives far away, but is always close to my heart."

Thirty Years Of Waiting For Real Love

Our paths crossed in the hall thirty years ago,
Not knowing that we would fall in love, years down the road.
A vision from the past came into view,
Of a young man in the hall coming to my rescue.

A rich kid with ego problems, knocked my books from my hand,
As I looked up into a face, there stood my superman.
A heavy crush I had, you might say was the word,
But my friends, called you a nerd.

Days passed by, you never looked my way,
Highschool ended, words I never got to say.
Life went on, a new life I began,
Never a thought of my superman.

Then one day, after a marriage or two,
I crossed the road, and there stood you.
Your name I spoke maybe once or twice,
We embraced one another, your arms felt so nice.

You wanted my number, you said let's keep in touch,
Nervous was I, my hand shook so much.
Later we met, you invited me in,
We talked about our children, life and friends.

Let's watch a movie, you said out of the blue,
I can't wait any longer, I have to kiss you.
So powerful the kiss, that set my soul afire,
With tears in my eyes, I'd never felt such desire.

I wanted to run, but I knew it was love,
You were sent to me by God, from Heaven above.
This is the story of a boy and a girl,
Thirty years later, living in this world.

We've been full circle with life can't you see,
Together now forever, my Superman and Me...

Brenda Bailey

"I would like to thank my husband... he is my inspiration."

A Dance

I danced with you slowly,
exploring your movements.

Our steps faltered as your
hand slipped from mine.

The tune echoes still
but where is my partner?

The ballad's charm, a promise
lost in sad confusion.

I had not mastered the waltz,
only discerned its unique grace.

Feeling our bodies sway,
in a promise of sweetness.

I am left dreaming...
the musicians gone home.

No partner to experience,
just a long haunting strain.

I will hum it softly,
alone in the enticement,

of what was to be -
a soft seductive tune.

Kimberlee Haines

"to my family who has shown me true love by example"

Honey, I'm Late

I'm feeling quite ill, I'm feeling quite blue;
I'm feeling really sad, is there a baby due?
I don't know how to explain it, What if I am?
I don't know how to be a mommy; I don't understand.
I took the precautions, and prayed for the best;
now it's time to drive to the store, and purchase the test.
I'm so scared and alone, will he care or will he roam?
I am only 19 and a baby myself,
I don't need a crib where once there was a shelf.

Merrie Wilbanks

Flower Among The Weeds

I'm glad I met you on life's rocky road
while gathering weeds grown from seeds I sowed
I pulled and I pulled till I thought I would drop
I must have had help when I planted that crop

I had to keep searching, through these useless plants
If I looked long enough, I might find, perchance
the seed I'd been saving, but somehow had lost
It must have been mixed with the seeds I tossed

I picked some wild roses, down life's winding way
I remember their fragrance still to this day
They withered and died, with my dreams and plans
and left me with nothing but thorns in my hands

I knew my one flower was blooming somewhere
and I knew no other could ever compare
I'd search and I'd search for all I was worth
If I had to pull every weed on this earth

That wonderful night, when you came to me
I'd have to be blind if I couldn't see
what now on my mind is forever engraved,
you're the flower that grew from the seed I saved

Now that we've met, from the search I resign
to devote all my life to making you mine
for I didn't find you, 'cause you weren't lost
and I merely can say, now our paths have crossed

The words, "make you mine," poor choice I suppose
'cause I can't pick you, like I'd pick a rose
but I'm truly hoping, I've found, indeed
my flower who'll grow with this lonely weed

Hal Gantt

Mr. & Mrs. Haid

In Dachau, each word of affection
scratched on scraps of paper,
slipped between guards
is an act of chivalry.

He gives her a silver heart pendant.
In return she gave him hope, a promise,
and a kiss; then hid the shiny metal
in a small tin beneath the boards
where she slept.

The two became survivors,
then man and wife; children born
after the war were told of dark times
ignited by flames of evil; where
two people reached out on the edge
of death as they were falling in love.

Susan Fridkin

"based on the life and love of Sonya Haid-Greene"

Child, Girl, Woman

Child, I said, Child -

Looking in caterpillars' faces up close,
Tall grass tickling your little nose,
Playing under the sun, carefree and wild,
Listening to the voices of monster trees,
Running, jumping, and chasing bees -
Child, I said, child.

Girl, I said, Girl -

Reading your books for hours on end,
Angry at people who would not bend,
Discovering lonely and merciless world,
Falling in love, painfully and with anguish,
Knowing not yet what is worth to cherish -
Girl, I said, girl.

Woman, I said, Woman -

Being spiritual and earthy in one,
Possessing powers yet staying calm,
Making sweet love to your Godsent man,
Bearing children and watching them grow,
Mastering sad art of letting go -
Woman, I said, woman.

Maria Y. Kurland

"*tempora mutantur et nos mutantur in illis*"

Elysium

And we moved, she and I
Opulent curiosity
Stirring shadows, torrid
Heat

And we danced, she and I
Absolute grace
Liquid souls, ravenous
Flame

And we loved, she and I
Furious passion
Rapturous union, delirious
Inferno

And we dreamed, she and I
Infinite serenity
Delicate spirits, tranquil
Embers

James H.K. Grannis

"for Sara, who shows me the magic with every smile..."

I Am Leaving

"I am leaving... Goodbye",
These are the words you'll hear me say,
On the eve of that sorry day.

I've put up with enough
And now it's time to get tough.
I don't need your words, your sorry excuses,
The games you played, the many abuses.

I've seen this game played before,
Now it's time to get to the core.
You know the rule,
Why are you on me like glue?

My times here were good,
To treat me well you could.
Yea, I'll miss your smile
But I will be happy, I don't cry.

You gave me everything,
You made me complete.
Now to pay you back,
that's the only feat.

My time is done,
and I am sorry to say
"I am leaving... goodbye",
Have a nice day!

Shawn Hayden Ramsingh

"we always find ourselves alone in this world; it's the inspiration inside of me that helps me grow."

The Journey

It begins
This quest for a mate
    With innocence
And continues
    With persistence
Some stop short
    They settle
Some go too far
    They didn't realize
Then there they are
The chosen few
    They know
For them the journey is done.

Danny Grubb

"for all of my friends who have found their soulmates."

Forever For Tonight

You place your hand
In the small of my back
Your warmth makes me feel
Like there's nothing I lack

We sway to the music
Your cheek to mine
You hold me so tenderly
As our souls entwine

The music fades
But you don't let go
You hold me here
While the lights dim low

You whisper "I love you"
Into my ear
And it seems as though
You've calmed every fear

We dance to the music
With the dim glow of light
I want this night to last forever
Yes, forever for tonight.

Caitlin R. Lee

Time Well Spent

i spend my time
just looking around
and around; when i see you
my eyes stop
halting in their place
seeing the beauty of your ears,
eyes and face
the subtle way you stand out
withdrawing me into your embodiment

i spend my time
every minute without you
wishing the opposite
wishing harder that i wasn't
all by myself
but reality slaps me in my face
bruising my heart
tender singed flesh of it
breaks and flops to the floor

i spend my time
tinkering in my brain
the propellers of my
imagination stir
and waken to spill my
confidential secrets
listen and don't hear
cover your senses to my callings

i spend my time
just listening
to every word you utter
they fall from your lips
like feathers
landing one by one
falling like raindrops
onto my pillow

i spend my time
dreaming, fantasizing
lifting my own clear hopes
head high
watching your every move

i spend it
wasting it
like old money in a cellar wall
i stand here
void as ever
waiting for you to notice me
my every breath to be yours
and what will never be
i still wish.....

Elyse Ford

My Noble Grandmother

She was kind and gentle, ever a smile or hug.
Always on the go, she was -- full of life and love.
Though time had taken its toll upon her brow,
The beauty of those eyes expressed the beauty of her soul.

I used to watch her as she cooked.
She showed me how she made her roast, slaw or lamb
Yet, mine has never tasted near so good.
It was that "flavor in her fingertips," I said.

I remember her visits to our house.
She'd drive up in her old Impala and
We'd run through the house and out the door.
"Granny's here!" What a feeling those words proclaimed!

Sundays were special as a child.
We gathered at my Granny's house
To eat the bounty she had prepared and
Bask in the glow of this humble, giving, noble mother.

Years have passed since then, yet the memories remain.
The tastes, the smells, the sounds linger as yesterday.
The piano still echoes with the touch of her hands.
My heart still feels the warmth of her embrace.

Today we celebrate her freedom from this mortal prison.
Last night her husband came to take her home.
No more pain, no more confusion, no more loneliness.
Now she's free to go and do and spread her wings once more.

Let us rejoice in the way she lived,
the way she loved and how she lives again!

Marnie L. Pehrson

"to my grandmother, Thelma B. White, born September 23, 1910, died August 2, 1999"

Faded Lust

Tears of black, falling forever
the depths of darkness rise
Worlds crashing and spinning
with passion of betrayal
Deep into the unknown with lust -
unfeeling the cold at every entrance
and exit and again and again
Winds from the East invade the space
of death as the rose is dropped
Casket buried deep and alone -
beyond imaginations, life returns
Seeds planted without cause and filled
with impurities, time and time again
death becomes a worldly cause
Faded Lust, unforgiven - dripped with
blood; it's over....

Merrie Wilbanks

Cinderella's Broken Slipper

Lovely ladies and honorable men:
Welcome, shall we let the gala begin?
Dance oh princess with your little toes,
dance with your prince,
that's how it goes...
Tap and tinkle,
her feet touch down...
yet no hint of sadness
in her silver French gown.
Blue eyes twinkle
and the party persists,
ladies and gentlemen locking wrists.
Sweet and tamed is the ball which turns,
the maids are humming
and dusting the urns.
All is going, all is well,
champagne fountain sprinkles
to continue our tale.
Innocence prevails and the children, so dear,
giggle unknowing and fondly they dance,
eyes so clear.
But, alas,
hear my entrance,
alas, all must go.
For everywhere I am
no happiness goes....

Elyse Ford

Our Little Picnics

when I was a child
for walks we would go
and so you could keep up
I would walk oh so slow

we'd walk through the garden
to check on the beans
then all through the field
I'd learn what love means

and down over the hill
we'd stop at the creek
you'd laugh out loud as
I bent down to peek

I'd peek at the fishies
all swimming down stream
that was so long ago
or to me it does seem

you spread out the blanket
we sat in the shade
and enjoyed the fine lunch
that we both had made

our picnics were fun
as they lasted each time
but now they are only
dear memories of mine

you since have passed on
you're in heaven above
having a picnic with God
and sharing the love

one day I pray
at a picnic we'll share
our love and the lunch
you always packed with such care.

Nancy Jones

"to my grandmothers whom I love very much."

Sweet & Yet... So Simple

A simple peck
A simple nudge
Sweet to the touch

A little bit wet
Tender and soft
Texture to want

Sometimes a dream
Sometimes a moment
A little bit of pleasure

In some dreams
In some reality
But always a desire

With a come hither
From afar
Those pouty lips
Make me quiver

In your absense I grow fonder
Of your warm and bittersweet kisses

It is no wonder I love you
For your kisses alone
Make my heart pitter-patter.

Monica Therese Curran

2:00am

I sit here at 2:00 AM, for want of sleep,
pondering memories coursing through my mind.
Suddenly a tear trickles down my cheek.
A quite unexpected event.
The wind is blowing outside,
making the chimes dance
and serenade me in their random musings.
No matter the hour,
when the chimes play,
I see sunny afternoons of days gone by.
Small pieces of the past
have come visiting me tonight.
Vignettes of my life as I knew it.
Ironic how such brief instances
that occurred so long ago
can carry such weight
in the scheme of what my mind
thinks is important enough to remember.
Or is it my heart that speaks now?
Short sweet moments of, for lack of a better word
I will call innocence.
The curiosities of love and youth
mingled with the discovery of sensuality.
Times when everything seemed to be so big.
When just a breath across my cheek
could set me on fire.
I can clearly see gentle fingers
not an inch from mine, not touching
but holding steady
as the energy of life
passed between them and my own.
Sometimes the memories are complete.
The moment to include the faces or sounds,
smells and tastes.

Others are just glimpses, caught
as if from the corner of my eye.
The sunlight glistening on a moist pair of lips
as I bent to kiss them.
The feel of hair as the wind caught it
and teased it against my brow.
The soft rise and fall of breathing
from the one I embraced.
There are so many precious pieces
in the puzzle of my life.
Not all are related to the love
or physical pleasures I've known,
but when those types do come to call,
I find myself enamored with them.
Perhaps it is the void of a gentle spirit
that causes me to recall the past
in such clarity.
In moments like these
I find the truest way to pay homage
to those who have made my life so rich,
is to tarry from my slumber
long enough to sit here
and give them remembrance on the page.
Lest there come a day
when age has hidden the paths in my mind
to those dear souls
who have chanced to dwell there awhile.

Kevin Drapela

The Light Inside

I left my home an innocent,
untouched, sweet, then summer set.
I was in a new world, all alone,
and to be secure I found
that to feel good about myself I had to
give up myself to be
the things that everyone expected of me.
I changed my looks, my style,
everything that was worthwhile,
to fit in with this new world of mine,
I lost a part of my inner sunshine.
I said I loved when only I lusted
for a time, a place,
a perfect life,
that I only could find behind closed eyes.
So I made mistakes and I gave myself away,
found that true love doesn't work that way,
and then I returned to the place I belong
and discovered that I wasn't all wrong,
Life isn't only a picnic or a song,
now I'm as happy as I ever needed to be.
I'm my own sun, the light in my life is me!

Lynette Webber

"*to all the loves in my life, enjoy - this is because of you!*"

Belong To Thee

You gave me a life to live,
You gave me breath to breathe,
You gave me a hug in times of despair,
You gave me love, to say you care.

The guidance you gave me through the bad times,
I will never again receive.
Your love that felt like the raindrops,
I shall never again feel.

For today I stand at your grave and see,
You're gone,
A life not lived complete,
Yet a life that's done.
You had so much ahead for you,
So much plans, so much dreams to come true
Why this all happened?
Remains in time due.

I still hear your laughter,
And for your dreams I shall never falter.
I still see your smile,
To this day heart has not beguile.

Through my life your dreams will come true,
And in my death I will finally see you.
I was so young when you left,
All I ever felt was neglect.

Your face remains like an angel to me,
To know the truth I must wait and see.
How fair is it for others to know you?
Yet the one who created me, I shall never know who?

You lived every day for me,
And always let things be.
You never let me down,
Even when all you could manage was a frown.

For the one that took you,
What shall I say?
You are the one I will ask on that day.

I hope you wait to see,
What a person I have turned out to be.
You gave me life to live,
You gave me breath to breathe,
And for that I belong to thee.

Shawn Hayden Ramsingh

> *"you can never move on from something until you put an end to the past."*

Ode To Feminism: Humankind Is Here

Mankind is gone, my fine young man
and Humankind is here.
Women don't just ride the bus
now they get to steer.

A policePerson will arrest you
while hiking up her skirt.
Despite the fact she squats to piss
you're still in a world of hurt.

The mailPerson now delivers
your letters every day.
But suddenly 'cause you like their legs
it doesn't mean you're gay.

It's a firePerson that will respond
and the firehose unroll,
only now you'll see pink panties when
they're sliding down the pole.

So give it up, my fine young man,
and offer them their due.
It's not so hard to articulate
from a proper point of view.

It's really not that big a thing
to acknowledge what they earn,
and demonstrate to them the fact
that even 'a man' can learn.

Bill Sterling

"to all my sisters everywhere..."

Butterflies Of Saturn

=+=+=+=+=+ Here are butterflies that skip
      Dull steps of metamorphosis

      No isolation in cocoons
   No gorging grubs like fat balloons

  Pure genesis on snow-kissed flowers
    Comes with no imperiled hours

    Their slow, eternal life begun
   Beneath a pink pearlescent sun

  Reflecting tints from rainbows born
  With pastel lights of endless dawn

Transcend through fabled time and myth
   To form the rings of Saturn's mist

Suzanne Delaney

"to Betty - fairies and bluebells remind me of you..."

Missed Connections

I watched her as she got up from her table.

She had sat three tables down from me
on the patio of a sidewalk café,
leisurely sipping an iced tea
and reading a small book.

She caught my eye when I turned my
head and saw her there by herself.
Something about her grabbed my focus.
Was it her shimmering amber brown hair
or was it those deeply beautiful eyes
that one couldn't help but get lost in?
Was it the way she sat, so demure and chaste?
Suddenly I realized just how divinely picturesque
she and the environment around her seem to be.
Surreal. Like a painting…... a work of art
come to life before me.

I watched her as she got up from her table.

As she walked off down the way,
I pondered to myself if I would ever see her again.
I wondered who she was,
where she was from and where she was going.
What if she had known who I was?
What if she knew the thoughts and aspirations
of that stranger that sat three tables up from her.
What if she was aware of the heart and soul
that lay hidden inside that unfamiliar man.
I watched her walk away and disappear around the corner.
What if she was the "one"?

I sighed and slipped a ten under a glass on the table.
I took a deep breath and got up to go on my way.

Three tables back, under the shade of the awning,
…she watched me as I got up from my table.

Tony Kinard

I Know

As I grow, learn and age
I learn to read people,
like writing on a page.

Faces changing familiar still,
emotions showing against your will.

I know what you're thinking.

Your body reveals to me,
emotions you wish would cease to be.

Lynette Webber

"to all the loves in my life, enjoy - this is because of you!"

A Blanket Full Of Dreams

One young couple in love
on a blanket just for two,
enjoying a lover's picnic
beneath a sky so blue.
They talk of the present
hope shining in their eyes,
dreaming of being together
never speaking of good-byes.
A few years down the road
now it's a blanket just for three,
enjoying a family picnic
beneath the apple tree.
They talk about the future;
how their child will grow,
wanting to pass on to her
the love they've come to know.
Years seem to pass so fast
now the blanket holds just one,
trying to find some warmth
beneath the morning sun.
She wraps the blanket around her
as memories soothe her pain.
Oh, how she longs for him;
aching to be in his arms again.
Her eyes grow tired and heavy
as she strokes their blanket of love.
She smiles as he carries her
to a blanket in heaven above.

Robyn Doersam

Fool Of Infiniti

Fool of Infiniti
A wanton bird pecks at the stars
A Jester peers through crystal bars
This prison of love in rainbow hue
Illusion parts to let you through

On dragon wings forever free
You quest into your dreams to see
Smoke and mirrors and shadow haze
To guide you through an endless maze

Slow motion tear rolls down her cheek
It's only passion that you seek
Engulfed in strange duality
She wonders her reality

Your eyes still mock her with desire
Your kisses light her inner fire
Your touch can melt her to your will
But you will never take your fill

Black widow spider guards your heart
She spun the web, she keeps it taut
It is your only fatal flaw
A secret, silent metaphor

And all about her swirl the dreams
The nightmares all with voiceless screams
And in her hand the strangest key
To fit the door of What Will Be

And when her eyes search yours again
You take her to the spider den
You spin the dreams she hopes to see
And lock your hearts in mystery

So enter in to lick the flame
Eternal prisoner of the game
Illusion is false imagery
She whispers your Infiniti

The Queen of Fate
The Queen of Fate by the outer Gate
Her carriage to Nowhere, will await
Her cloak is wrapped against the night
Her eyes are wide with peculiar fright

Gray horses eyes turn back in fear
With thunderclaps upon her ear
Blue jagged lightning points the way
Along the path to yesterday

Cold, sullen driver cracks his whip
His crooked smile curls round his lip
His horses leap the cruel abyss
Dark Queen of Fate sees none amiss

Above the mist a gate appears
Who will wipe the Gate-man's tears ?
Gray horses strike and paw the air
Fate Queen ascends the carriage stair

And all about her swirl the dreams
The nightmares all with voiceless screams
And in her hand a wondrous key
To lock Enigma's Mystery

Pass through the gate O Queen of Fate
Another carriage will await
Drawn by Steeds of Promises
Illusion Starts and Finishes.

Suzanne Delaney

Under All That

Hunger, disease, and death raid the planet;
tearing it to pieces, like a pack of wolves on a steak.
How can they say someone controls all this?
How can they tell me this person is good?
Under all that, if you look a little deeper,
you see more than just destruction.

Hope, dreams, and happiness lay there;
starting a new life, like the springtime flowers.
How can they say there's no such thing as second chances?
How can they tell me there's no new beginnings?
Under all that, if you start over,
you see more than just wishes.

Flowers, sunsets, and angels are honorable in the heart;
bringing glory into this life, like a smile on a child's face.
How can they say I reach too high?
How can they tell me there's no true love?
Under all that, if you look at the core,
you see more than what's there.

Best friend and love shines through everything;
glowing into the hate, like the moon in the darkness.
How can they say I am crazy for dreaming?
How can they tell me it's only in my mind?
Under all that, if you don't judge,
you see more.
I see more.

Katie Backus

"to my best friend, Krystle, you are like my sister!"

Starting Anew

i lay on my side of the bed
wanting to be held
i don't know where we went wrong
i only know we failed

i ache for the attention
i crave to be touched
i never really knew
i'd miss it this much

i want to get away
and try to find a life
i can't always be here
pretending to be his wife

but it is so hard
when you've never been apart
i don't want to hurt him
i don't want to break his heart

but i feel like if i stay
i'll never know what's there
i want to have my own place
 i just don't know how or where

Debbie Gooch

"to my mom"

The Screen

I listen to the
words you write
and read them
on a screen

I wonder if
the things you
feel are really
what you mean

It seems sometimes
that when we talk
I sometimes strike
a nerve

quick exits mean
you need an out
a way to dodge
or swerve

I listen to the
things you say
and wonder what
you feel

we laugh we talk
this ain't TV
we interact
it's real

Emerson Dawson

Portraits

If I could paint you, and you could paint me,
and whatever we painted was the way we would be,
in the great masterpiece I'd paint of you,
I'd paint you to look just the way that you do.
One change I would make, I would never forget,
but I'm not quite ready to tell you just yet.

And how would you paint me? I'm afraid to ask,
for painting me handsome would be quite some task.
But I know you could do it, I know 'cause you see,
you have to remember, this is my fantasy.
As you let your brush fly, one thing I would pray,
that you'd never paint me fore'er gone away.

The brightest of stars I'd take from the skies,
a permanent twinkle for your lovely eyes.
To light up your life, and brighten your days,
I'd mix in my paints, some of sun's golden rays,
soft shimmering moonlight to highlight your style.
All men who beheld you, would stare for a while.

So you'd always feel good, I'd paint in the wind
to gently caress you and cool down those men.
Now you may be thinking, there's no way, he can't,
for where would he ever find the right paint,
but I hold the pen, my thoughts to disperse,
that gives me access to the whole universe.
Therefore is naught that I cannot do
to enchance this lovely portrait of you.

Wherever your heart went, that's where you'd be,
the background would change with your mood, you see.
No place in the world would be out of reach,
if the seaside should beckon, you'd be on a beach.
You might look one time and be in the mountains,
the next perhaps gazing on Rome's lovely fountains.

No artist or paints could possibly add,
they can only show things you always had.
So all these enhancements, unneeded, it seems,
for just as you are, so you are in my dreams.
The one change I'd make that I mentioned before
would lift up my heart to where eagles soar.
'Cause down deep inside, where eyes cannot see,
I'd paint you forever, in love with me.

Hal Gantt

"to lovers everywhere"

Baby's Blessing

A baby to hold,
A baby to keep,
A baby to love,
Awake or asleep.

A baby to rock,
A baby to feed,
Relying on you
To fill every need.

A baby to teach,
A spirit to mould,
For wisdom is much
More precious than gold.

There will be trials,
There will be tears,
So always remember,
Trust God through the years.

Julia M. Zwicker

Closing Doors

You opened your door
and ushered me in,
tempting me with visions of
what might have been.

I spent what seemed forever
on your threshold, in pain...
one foot out, one foot in,
and my heart in between.

I paced and I pondered
what was taking so long,
and tried to find out,
from you, what was wrong.

When I finally realized
I was in the wrong place,
I stepped outside and
closed the door in your face.

The sound the door made
could barely be heard,
but that doesn't matter
'cause my heart said the word...

Good-bye.

Alanna Webb

ABOUT THE POETS

The publisher wishes to thank all of the poets for permission to reprint their copyrighted works. Copyright of these individual poems is held by the individual poets. Contact the poets by email by visiting http://www.lovestories.com/templates/volume1.cfm

Charles Albano

Amun-Ra is a former journalist, photographer and instructor of English. He still teaches English part-time at a Dallas university. His journalism work have been featured in the Wichita Eagle, Tulsa Tribune, Kansas City Star as well as numerous poetry magazines.

Katie Backus, 14, Berlin, CT, is a swimmer, ballet dancer, and a poet. She writes to express her feelings.

Brenda Bailey, author of romance, mystery and inspirational books, gives her husband, Larry, all the credit for her writing. Writing is her passion, which used to be therapy, but now is a job that she enjoys very much.

B.W. Behling, 43, Wescosville, PA, is a native New Yorker, transplanted to Pennsylvania Dutch Country after a devastating fire left him homeless an penniless. He now shares a rich and wonderful life with Donna, his beloved soulmate and guiding light.

Kelsey Blackmore

Bob Brokaw is just a country boy from North Carolina. All of his poems are about people and events of his lifetime.

Butterfly Dreams (aka Jerry O. Jordan) is a general contractor in Scottsville, VA. An avid skydiver, he believes poetry is an outlet for emotions, hidden by the callouses of man.

C. Elizabeth, 21, Pennsylvania, recently developed a passion for poetry in the Summer of 1999, after being inspired by a special someone. She believes that even if a love is unrequited, it still brings its fair amount of sunshine

Sheila Cadilli is a native Californian - a nature lover with a reverence for life, passion for poetry, and a weakness for light-hearted limericks.

Lydia Castilho of Torrance, CA, is a retired aerospace staff assistant. She is married, has five children and three grandsons. She has written five novels, short stories and poetry, and enjoys sharing her creative endeavors

Jerry Chiccarine, Norristown, PA, was born and raised in the Perkiomen Valley He grew up by the creek on the edge of the woods, surrounded by nature. Early in his tumultuous childhood, he began pouring his passion for everything into his writing.

Jim Culhane, 32, Houston, TX, is a novice poet who only recently became interested in writing. He has obtained Microsoft™ Certified Systems Engineer & Internet certification and is beginning a career in e-commerce

Monica Therese Curran, 28, Tracy, CA, works full-time and is a part-time student who loves her husband, Scott, dearly and their two kittens, Sassy and Sunshine. She's been writing poetry since grade school. Poetry is her passion, and her poetry has been published in quarterlies and anthologies.

T.J. Daniels writes poetry and dreams of the day when he can move to the beautiful countryside.

Emerson Dawson

John Dee says, "All of my literary works are a gift from God. Thank you, reader, and may you keep on smiling!"

Suzanne Delaney, 49, is a registered nurse, currently not practising. She now has time to pursue her interest in writing poetry and believes that poetry i a healing force, a creative power that can touch the collective consciousness, inspiring new insights into love and peace.

Dhynah is a lifelong resident of Milwaukee, WI, and a former medical secretar who now enjoys writing poetry.

Robyn Doersam is married with two children. She has been writing poetry as long as she can remember. Her sense of accomplishment is if her poetry soothes someone or makes even one person smile.

Kevin Drapela

Paula Duquette, 30, Mazon, IL, is the devoted mother of two children, Alex and Lauren, and their dog Anna. She has been writing poetry since she was thirteen years old, and it is still her favorite outlet.

Dale A. Edmands, Andover, MA, began writing in his childhood. He has written two poetry books, and has received numerous local and national awards. In 1996, he read his poem, "Sixteen Years in Andover," at the close of the town's 350th Anniversary. The poem resides in the town's time-capsule. He shares a hundred year-old Cape with his wife, Linda, their two children, Hannah and Douglas, three cats, and Maggie, a Black Lab. He is webmaster for Kookamonga Square, an award-winning poetry site at http://www.geocities.com/Paris/Tower/9556.

Brent (Bobo) Faust, 23, Westfield, IA, currently works at Gateway Computers as a phone technician. He fathers a beautiful daughter named Lizzy May Faust. He has been writing poetry since his sophomore year and has been hooked ever since.

Elyse Ford, 15, Oklahoma, is a newly aspiring poet who lives with her parents and younger sister. Since the 7th grade, she has expressed her emotions through her poetry.

D.L. Frantz, 45, Wescosville, PA, is a water quality specialist. Her passion is sharing thoughts with the hope of evoking emotions common among the warm-hearted. D.L. has been writing since her early teens. "It began as a sort of therapy to ease me through puberty and has now hopefully evolved as a means of inspiring emotions and provoking thoughts in such a manner that we, the human race, can recognize our similarities, thus enabling us to love each other on our way to a common destiny."

Susan Fridkin is a Midwest poet whose poetry has been published in numerous poetry presses and anthologies. Recent magazine publications include MIDSTREAM and the CCAR JOURNAL. Currently she is working on a second chapbook in tribute to the Jews and *Righteous Gentiles* of the Holocaust, The Poem Remembers.

Hal Shuford Gantt is a retired correctional food service manager. He likes to write poetry on a wide variety of topics that inspire him, for the enjoyment of anyone who likes his style of writing.

Emily Garcia (Angel), 16, The Colony, TX, is a highschool junior. She enjoys participating in theatre, band, OM, and her chuch youth group. She has been writing since the age of twelve.

Debbie Gooch, 37, Berea, KY, is an assistant manager for a retail store. She has three children, and loves to write poetry.

James H.K. Grannis

Grey Winds lives near Pittsburgh, PA, and is planning to attend a local university for a degree in theatrical directing. He has written numerous poems and have had a few published.

Frank Grima, aka Max The Poet(c), 35, lives in Littleton, NH, with his daughter, McKenzie Rose. He has spent the last two years of his life writing romantic poetry. Inspired by his search for his soulmate, and the beauty of the White Mountains, Max has won many awards for his poetry. His poetry is used widely on the Internet. His wish is that every reader enjoy every word while sharing his love for life.

Danny Grubb, 20, Seattle, WA, moved to the United States from Berlin, Germany, at age eleven. He discovered poetry at age fourteen and has been writing ever since. He is attending Shoreline Community College.

Kimberlee Haines

Pauline Hamblin, 41, Ohio, works full-time as a registered nurse. She only recently started to write poetry. Her hobbies include collecting Barbie dolls, Hot Wheels and playing with her three year-old son.

C.J. Heck, a native Ohioan, now lives in New Hampshire where she is a wife, mother of three grown daughters, and a new grandma. Besides poetry, she writes fiction, non-fiction, and short stories for children. Her publishing credits include, *Barking Spiders and Other Such Stuff*, (SterlingHouse Publisher, Inc.), March 2000, and other works published in St. Anthony Messenger and TOUCHSTONE, a quarterly publication of the Poetry Society of New Hampshire.

Tammy S. Hoover

Basi Hummel is Swiss and an incurable free spirit by nature. She has traveled to many places and has met many people. She began to write short stories and poetry as a child. Christianity is her root and without it, she would truly be homeless.

Bryana Johnson, 17, lives in a small town named Fargo in Georgia. She has been writing poetry since she has been old enough to hold a pen. Poetry is her passion, although she does write a few short stories.

Nancy Jones, Berea, KY, is a full-time homemaker. She enjoys spending time with her husband and her family. She writes poetry to express her feelings and opinions. She loves sharing her poetry.

Tony Kinard

Maria Y. Kurland, born in Russia, has been living in the United States for ten years. Married, an artist by education, she has been writing poetry as a hobby. As with painting, writing helps her express her emotions.

Caitlin R. Lee, 17, is a highschool student in Medicine Hat, Alberta, Canada, living with her family. She collects and writes poetry because of her deep infatuation with it.

Anthony Limes, 40, Ridgely, TN, is a single parent who loves writing poetry. He believes that writing poetry is a gift from God, and should be shared with everyone. If he can touch just one person with a poem, he will consider himself a success.

Tammy Lively-Sellers, 33, resides in Murphysboro, IL, with her boyfriend, Gary, and their five children. She has been writing since she was eleven, and encourages her children to write.

Randall Longshore

Robert L. Macchia, 52, Long Island, NY, has been married for 28 years, has three daughters and one son. Poetry is his #1 passion after his family, two parrots and a cat.

Brenda Mae, 38, Ohio, is married with three children. She has been writing poetry for 18 months. She loves reading and writing poetry.

Grace Martino is the mother of a beautiful sixteen year-old daughter and loves writing poetry as well as short stories, and has even written a novel. She hopes to someday be a published writer.

Andrea L. Michano, 31, Ojibways of Pic River First Nation, enjoys spending time with her family, writing, drawing and almost anthing creative. She thinks that the people in Pic River are simply the best!

J.C. Monterrosa, twenty-something, resides in Nashville, TN, all by his little self. He loves knowledge, arts and sciences, sword fighting, and so much more. Though single, he longs to live in a castle with the woman to whom many of his poems are directed.

Jim Morton, 42, Palm City, FL, has been writing poetry since the second grade. He also plays guitar and puts some of his words to music. He enjoys the challenge of trying to put the feelings of the heart onto paper.

Dave Nieman, 16, is a junior in highschool. He has been writing poetry since 1995, and poetry is very much a part of his life now. He also enjoys reading, writing stories, gardening, and listening to classic rock.

Marnie Pehrson, 33, of Georgia is a wife and mother of five. She's a writer and Internet strategist who enjoys writing poetry centering around her religious (LDS) beliefs. Marnie highlights other writers and professionals in her Web projects found at http://www.pwgroup.com.

Sunny Pierce

Amanda Piotrowski, 22, Ohio, is a disabled housewife who spends time with her husband, Tim, and their bird, Cairo. Poetry is an outlet and inspiration.

Bob Pool presently resides in Margate, NJ, employed by Baley's Casino in Atlantic City as a bell captain. All of his poems are published in his book entitled, *Poems of Assorted Flavors*.

Chuck Pool is retired from the United States Air Force. He graduated from the University of Maryland, and is married to Paige. Most of his poetry has been published in a book entitled, *One Rhyme At A Time*.

Martha Powell-Mitchell is currently a full-time student seeking teacher certification in elementary education. Poetry is one of her varied interests, including music, dance, and computers. The mother of six is also actively involved in church and school organizations. She and her family reside in the rural community of Kirkmansville, KY.

Odessa Lynette Price, 19, Arizona, has always wanted to share her poetry with others. Poetry has been a passion, and improves when she has someone special to direct her words to; everyone needs an inspiration. She works by day, and writes by night, when the stars reach the ends of the earth.

Shawn Hayden Ramsingh is an aspiring creative writer, who enjoys writing poetry that expresses emotion. His readers take an emotional journey and are left to make their own interpretation.

Carrie Reger, 56, widow of four years, lives in southern West Virginia. She loves to sing country gospel, and writes songs and poetry.

Renée Rose, 41, from Montreal, Canada, is a self-employed writer/composer seeking to market her music. "It's never too late to live your dreams."

Brenda Swanberg, 25, Mountlake Terrace, WA, is pursuing a career in law enforcement. With tremendous support from family and friends, she has hopefully reached her goal by the time this book is published. Many thanks to Angie, her best friend, and to MJ, the love of her life.

John Henry Scott is a stage and film actor, magician, radio personality clown and bass guitar player. He has written a full-length play, songs, and poetry for special occasions. His pen was still for many years until he met Jan, a special lady who convinced him to start writing again.

Maurice Sherry is a US Navy veteran who enjoys poetry, cats, computing, singing, and nice people.

Christopher A. Smith, 27, Stallings, NC, is a father of a six year-old daughter. He enjoys writing for the pleasure of others.

Rod Smith

Tony Spivey, 41, is a middle school teacher in North Carolina. Poetry is his passion, and provides an outlet to express his deepest thoughts. Tony is married and has one daughter, Brandy, who is the light of his life.

Bill Sterling, the pen name of Bill Fish, Jr., resides in Buchanan, MI, and Chandler, AZ.

Kathleen Kerry Swanson, 19, Clearwater, FL, is a full-time college student majoring in education. She has dreamed of being a teacher for as long as she can remember, which is also as long as she has been writing poetry to truly express herself.

Michael J. Tripp, 25, Anchorage, AK, is a commercial airline pilot who owes all his poetic inspiration to his lovely Brenda.

Julia Warfel, 23, is a photographer in central Florida. She attended Hollins College and the University of Florida. In addition to writing poetry, Julia loves to ride her horses, play music and dance.

Alanna Webb, 38, Broken Arrow, OK, is a single romantic-at-heart. Her poetry included herein is the first she's written since high school. She was inspired by all the wonderful poets at Lovestories.com, the site she founded in 1997. She has discovered that to write a good poem you have to really open yourself up to your emotions.

Lynette Webber lives with her family in Michigan's Upper Peninsula, and currently attends highschool. She participates in band and drama activities.

Merrie Wilbanks, 19, Orlando, FL, is an honest woman just trying to make her place in the world. Poetry is her release.

Wintersong, 65, lives in Arlington, Washington.

Sandra Wommack, 42, Forest, VA, is a registered nurse who has been married for twenty years and has six children. Her passion for writing poetry is an expression of her innermost thoughts and feelings.

Julia Zwicker, Canada, is a student pursuing a writing career. She is a Christian, and values family and friends. She writes poetry, fantasy, and fiction.

Careful effort has been made to trace the copyright ownership of all poems in this anthology and to obtain the necessary permissions to reprint. If any error or omission has occurred, it is completely unintentional, and the publisher will make necessary corrections in future printings provided that written notification is made to: Backup Computer Resources, 905 S. 30th St., Broken Arrow, OK 74014.

INDEX OF POETS

A

Charles Albano 7
Amun-Ra 77

B

Katie Backus 136
Brenda Mae 34
Brenda Bailey 104
B.W. Behling 10
Kelsey Blackmore 16
Bob Brokaw 47, 82
Butterfly Dreams 13, 38

C

C. Elizabeth 20
Sheila Cadilli 12
Lydia Castilho 39
Jerry Chiccarine 3, 17
Jim Culhane 69, 80
Monica Therese Curran 122

D

T. J. Daniels 2, 79
Emerson Dawson 138
John Dee 48, 53
Suzanne Delaney 129, 134
Dhynah 54, 66
Robyn Doersam 133
Kevin Drapela 123
Paula Duquette 4, 92, 101

E

Dale Edmands 65, 98

F

Brent Clayton Faust 23, 67
Elyse Ford 94, 115, 119
D. L. Frantz 52, 60
Susan Fridkin 109

G

Hal Gantt 108, 139
Emily Garcia 22, 43
Debra Gooch 137
James H.K. Grannis 111
Grey Winds 6, 50
Frank Grima 74
Danny Grubb 103, 113

H

Kimberlee Haines 106
Pauline Hamblin 31
C.J. Heck 1, 19, 96
Tammy S. Hoover 32
Basi Hummel 44

J

Bryana Johnson 27
Nancy Jones 120

K

Tony Kinard 130
Maria Y. Kurland 110

L

Caitlin R. Lee 114
Anthony Limes 72, 85
Tammy Lively-Sellers 58
Randall Longshore 24, 94

M

Robert L. Macchia 35
Grace Martino 28
Max The Poet© 74
Amanda Michano 62
J.C. Monterrosa 70
Jim Morton 40, 64, 99

N

Dave Nieman 49

P

Marnie L. Pehrson 117
Sunny Pierce 57
Amanda Piotrowski 61
Bob Pool 18
Chuck Pool 8
Martha Powell-Mitchell 15
Odessa Lynette Price 89

R

Shawn Hayden Ramsingh 112, 126
Carrie Reger 5, 14
Renée Rose 42

S

Christopher A. Smith 59, 73
John Henry Scott 88
Maurice Sherry 87
Rod Smith 26, 100
Tony Spivey 36
Bill Sterling 128
Brenda Swanberg 45
Kathleen Kerry Swanson 56, 75, 76

T

Michael J. Tripp 46

W

Julia Warfel 86, 90, 102
Alanna Webb 142
Lynette Webber 125, 132
Merrie Wilbanks 107, 118
Wintersong 41, 63
Sandra Wommack 93

Z

Julia M. Zwicker 141

ABOUT THE EDITOR

Alanna Webb spent eight years as a chemical engineer before jumping offtrack to pursue her interest in computers. She taught herself how to create graphics and web pages, and has created web sites since the web went mainstream.

Alanna found a way to combine her computer skills with her love of romance when she founded Lovestories.com in September of 1997, creating one of the largest love and romance communities on the Internet. Lovestories.com has been recognized worldwide by media and organizations, including USA TODAY, LA TIMES, ENTERTAINMENT WEEKLY, ABCNEWS.COM, CNN.COM, HOUSTON CHRONICLE and YAHOO!.

She lives in Broken Arrow, Oklahoma, is single, and still believes in marriage for life... she just needs to find her soulmate.

LOVESTORIES.COM POETRY COMMUNITY

- Sign-up for our free Poet Account.
- Log in anytime to post poems you have written.
- Your poetry could be featured in our future anthologies.
- Meet other poets... become part of our community.
- Weekly and monthly contests.
- Visit and enjoy poetry every day.

Our poets enjoy receiving comments about their poetry. You may contact the poets included in this volume by visiting:
http://www.lovestories.com/templates/volume1.cfm

To Order More Books:

Call Our Distributor at (800) 431-1579 or us at (918) 258-7669

Online Ordering Information at:
http://www.lovestories.com/templates/volume1.cfm